An Illustrated Resource Guide For
Shallow Water Wells

DIG YOUR OWN
WELL

Daniel Schoeman

Art production and Book design by A.D. Schoeman.
Cover design and Ilustration by A.D. Schoeman.
All illustrations done by A.D. Schoeman and the Inkscape Openclipart project.

Note To Readers.
The information provided in this book is designed to provide helpful information on the subjects of water management. This book is a reference guide presented solely for educational and entertainment purposes. The author and publisher are not offering it as professional services advice. While best efforts have been used in preparing this book, the author and publisher make no representations or warranties of any kind and assume no liabilities of any kind with respect to the accuracy or completeness of the contents and specifically disclaim any implied warranties of merchantability or fitness of use for a particular purpose. No warranties or guarantees are expressed or implied by the publisher's choice to include any of the content in this volume. Neither the publisher nor the individual author shall be liable for any physical, psychological, emotional, financial, or commercial damages, including, but not limited to, special, incidental, consequential or other damages. Our views and rights are the same: You are responsible for your own choices, actions, and results. References are provided for informational purposes only and do not constitute endorsement of any websites or other sources. Readers should be aware that the websites listed in this book may change.

Copyright © 2019 Daniel Schoeman
All rights reserved.
ISBN-13: 978-0-6398054-1-2

"Plans to protect air and water, wilderness and wildlife are in fact plans to protect man."

- Stewart Udall

Contents

1. Foreword
2. Chapter 1: The Origin of Water.................01
   - The Water Cycle............................03
   - Conservation...............................08
3. Chapter 2: Finding a Water Source For Your Land..13
   - Public water...............................15
   - Alternative Sources........................19
4. Chapter 3: Water From The Ground............25
   - Well Basics................................26
   - The Soil...................................29
   - The Water Table............................31
   - Planning...................................32
   - PVC Pipe Drills............................36
   - Construct Your Drill.......................42
   - How To.....................................51
   - Conclusion.................................59
   - Auger Drilling.............................62
   - How To.....................................63
   - How To Make a Well Screen..................68
   - Well Points................................72
   - How To.....................................73
   - Conclusion.................................80
   - Dug Wells..................................82
   - Preparations...............................86

- How To...89
- Conclusion..97
- Summary..98

5. Chapter 4: Basics of Wells & Water Pumps.101
    - Pump Basics......................................103
    - Pitless Adapters................................107
    - Basics of Shallow Well Jet Pumps..........108
    - Basics of a Deep Well Jet Pump.............111
    - Basics of a Submersible Deep Well Jet Pump
     113
    - Connecting a Solar Water Pump............116
    - General Pump Maintenance..................122
    - Conclusion..124
    - Home Water Treatment Setup...............125

6. Chapter 5: The Basics of Managing a Well. 129
    - Protect your well................................130
    - Call an Expert....................................131
    - Visual Inspections..............................133
    - Disinfecting a Well.............................136

7. Glossary of Terms..................................145

8. About The Author..................................148

Foreword

When we discuss well water in this book, we are referring to *Shallow Water Wells (10-50 feet)*. **We recommend thoroughly testing the water extracted from your property before you consider drinking it or using it for any application.** We live in a time where contaminants are present in all forms of water and they pose a serious health hazard. Depending on where you are in the world, you will find that most shallow water wells produce water that is only good for irrigation and cleaning purposes.

New Projects and Common sense

- Safety is everything! Whether you dig, install, buy, modify or remove, remember to use your common sense and to put safety first.

Safety applies not just to you, but to children, visitors, workers, livestock, pets and wild animals.

- Follow local laws and regulations and avoid unwanted attention. Keep everything legal and obtain permits where needed.

You have enough on your plate as it is.

- Buy quality. If it sounds too cheap, it probably is. Avoid tanks, filters and pumps imported from countries known for their cheap prices. Why take a chance on something that's function is to keep you alive?

Example: Use Schedule 40 PVC pipe and avoid

the thinner, cheaper selections.

- Every storage container, no matter how big or small, must be food grade quality or have a food grade liner on the inside.

Don't use any container that was previously used for chemical storage.

- Know how to repair and maintain all systems related to water on your property.

Keep spare parts.

- Always have a backup plan. Pumps use electricity. What will you do when there's no power? Be prepared for any worst-case scenario.

- Test your water!

Whether from a lake, river, well or rooftop, always have it tested.

If unsure about the presence of pathogens, boil it. Never assume anything. Always have a water test kit at hand. They are reliable, inexpensive and simple to use.

When in doubt, test first!

- Make nice with your neighbors.

Communities create a network of trust and cooperation. Try to find like-minded people in the community and reach out to them.

This is not just about getting, but also about giving.

- Research.

Don't take resources for granted. Use the websites provided by government agencies that are responsible for environmental protection, disease control and water management.

CHAPTER 01

Understanding The Origin Of Water

The blue planet. As seen from space, our planet is an attractive blue ball, wrapped in water and covered in a web of clouds. It is easy to become mesmerized by the appeal that the oceans, rivers and lakes have, for those are the very places where humans chose to settle and to start civilizations. Innately, every human being is aware of the possibilities that water can create; it is the very source of life that we have come to depend and to rely on.

For billions of years, tiny drops have been migrating in an endless cycle round and round the earth. Minute little molecules have traveled as droplets, from the oceans to the clouds, across the land, and down into rivers and lakes and into the ground. This constant movement of droplets, from solid to liquid to gaseous states, is what's known as the Water Cycle.

Our fauna and flora have come to depend on these droplets that circulate the planet, to the extend that nothing on earth can survive without it. When we look at the water cycle, we quickly realize something very important. Water, or its absence, represents the absolute most important resource known to man, and it has been a part of our planet from the beginning of time. The water in my glass, has been traveling nonstop, since before the age of the dinosaurs. It's fallen as a drop of rain in the Sahara, as a torrential monsoon in India, a flash-flood in Arizona or become part of a glacier in Canada. It has never ceased to exist; it has merely taken on a different state of existence.

Water cycles exist in a state of balance and provide us with the fundamental basics that we need to understand droughts, floods and extreme weather patterns. As landowners, we have to become experts at understanding the inner workings of the water cycle on our planet. If there is one thing that space exploration has taught us, it's that a planet without water is completely uninhabitable.

When we look at our planet we have to ask ourselves, why do only some planets have water and where does this water come from? Currently there are two theories related to the origins of water on planet Earth.

The older and more established theory states that water was possibly carried all the way across the universe through comets and meteorites.

A newer, and also very plausible theory states that water has been a part of this planet from the beginning. Whatever the case, it is correct to assume that the vast majority of the water on planet earth has been here for millions of years.

Of concern for landowners, and owners of self-sufficient homesteads, is making sure that we understand the "water cycle" and how it applies to us and our immediate environment.

The Water Cycle

We are all familiar with the classic water cycle (a.k.a. the hydrological cycle) that

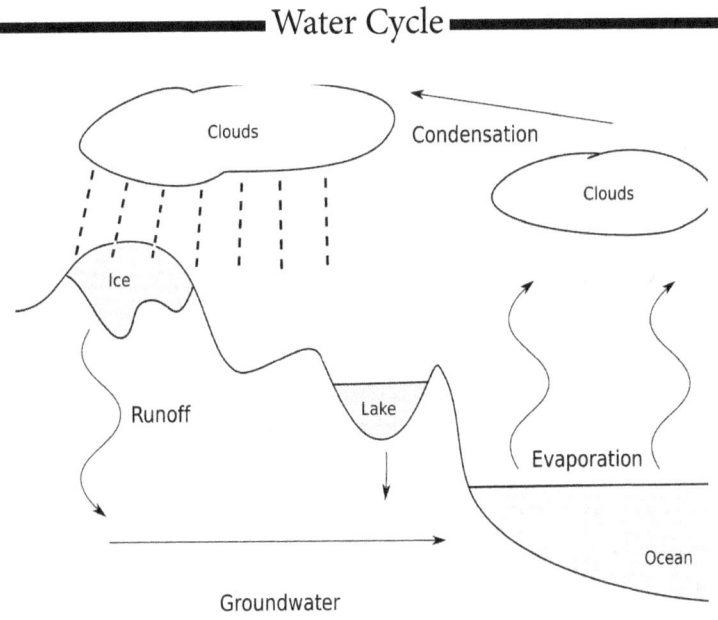

Liquid water > Evaporation > Condensation > Precipitation > Runoff/ flow back to the original state

we learned about as youngsters.

1. The cycle starts with the evaporation of water from the surface of the ocean.

2. The moist air rises up and it starts to cool down.

3. This water vapor condenses and it forms clouds.

4. Clouds filled with moisture are moved all around the globe and the moisture returns to the surface as precipitation (rain). Not only does the rain form lakes and rivers, but the rain also replenishes groundwater deep inside the earth.

(Take note that this is the very system that we mimic in water distillation and filtration systems.)

What makes the water cycle really interesting is the fact that we call this a "closed hydrological system". It is a closed system, because the amount of water on the planet does not fluctuate. Yes, it can be broken down and reformed through various chemical processes, but there is no significant input or output of water to or from the planet.

Where does it go, you might ask, in times of drought?

The simple answer is: *Somewhere else.*

In theory, when there is a drought in one part of the world, there will be floods in other parts. Abundance over yonder, means scarcity over here. It is a balanced system that is in constant flux. Water does not disappear, it just moves with the weather systems and returns as precipitation when conditions permit.

Let's look at a breakdown of where, and in what forms, water is found:

- **96%** of water accumulates on the earth's crust. This is the water present in reservoirs like the oceans, lakes, seas and rivers.

- **2%** is found in a solid state in the ice caps, glaciers and mountain caps.

- **1.7%** is found as groundwater inside the crust.

Global Water Crisis

- Droughts caused by extreme weather events are destroying agriculture and displacing people. Waves of migrants are fleeing areas ravaged by droughts.

- Population growth has increased the need for water and also released more contaminants into existing groundwater sources.

- The demand for more food is putting stress on groundwater reserves.

- Weak infrastructure is not able to cope with the demand and most countries are in dire need of new technology to solve the water crisis.

- **0.001%** is found in the atmosphere and air around us as clouds, falling rain and water vapor.

At first glance, the above-mentioned statistics might seem pretty decent. The percentage (96%) of water found on the surface crust seems to favor man's chances of survival.
But how much of this water is actually potable freshwater?
The answer is quite disturbing.
Only about 2.5% of this water is freshwater. Add to that the fact that most of this freshwater is frozen as ice, and suddenly we are looking at a figure of only 0.65 %, which represents the earth's total water supply that is neither salty nor frozen.
The moral of the story?
Right now, water is absolutely the most precious resource on earth!

The tiny percentage of 0.65, represents the possibility of life on our planet and we humans are scrambling to safeguard ourselves from running out.
The National Geographic Society calls it "Water Wars" and states that underground water is pumped so aggressively around the globe that land is sinking, civil wars are being waged and agriculture is being transformed.
Right now, the city of Beijing is sinking at a rate of 4 inches per year, due to the depletion of the groundwater underneath.
The water cycle teaches us that we cannot pump water from wells more rapidly than they

Water and Droughts

Surface water is freshwater found above ground that accumulates in nature through precipitation. Once this water penetrates the soil, it gets filtered down into aquifers that store groundwater.

A large portion of the freshwater on earth is lost through runoff to the oceans.
When a period of abnormally dry weather endures in a region, it can create an imbalance that causes a drought.

We can identify four typical drought scenarios.

• Rain events - When there is a shortage in local precipitation.

• Moisture content of soil - If conditions arise that causes the soil to lack the moisture necessary to sustain a particular crop.

• Water levels - When the surface water and groundwater levels are

both below normal.

• Supply - When the demand for water cannot be met through the supply infrastructure.

can be replenished. We rely on precipitation runoff to replenish our groundwater. This is a very important aspect of the water cycle, since more than 30% of the planet's fresh water (in liquid form) is groundwater. We all want to share in this resource, but first we will have to familiarize ourselves with the location, depth and quality of groundwater in our area. Water is not an infinite resource and to avoid complications, we will have to learn how to manage and conserve this resource.

You might need *X amount* of water for your land, but if every neighbor in your area is extracting water from the same aquifer, things can take a turn for the worse. Imagine a bottle with 15 straws in it. The bottle will be empty in seconds.

If, during one summer, we have fewer rain events that usual, that groundwater aquifer will not be replenished and we could potentially sit with a dry well.

This is the reality as more and more people are drilling wells and extracting groundwater.

Conservation

There is a good chance, that you have very good water just a few feet underneath your land and if so, you will be eager to drill a well. That's your right to do so, but be aware that besides just drilling a well, you also might have to change your lifestyle and your opinions about sustainability.

Traditionally, homestead owners have always

required large quantities of **water for irrigation and livestock**. If we look at the present evidence as seen through the water cycle, we quickly start to realize that the perceived abundance of water is an illusion. In certain areas the situation is deteriorating rapidly and we will have to adapt and evolve with it. This could mean that some of us will have to start thinking about scaling down.

If the supply cannot cover the demand, we will have to change on our end. This is already happening all over the world in many first world countries. Farmers are looking at alternative agriculture practices that can still secure a high yield, but that utilize less land and less water. This is definitely possible and actually recommended by the experts.

Make the right decision and start thinking about water conservation on your property.

Consider some of the following options:

- **Scaling down on irrigation.** Drip irrigation reduces evaporation and saves huge amounts of water. Timers can schedule irrigation for the cooler parts of the day.

- **Create a water-rich vegetation** with low water needs.

- **Recycle your house's grey water.** This is something that every human on the planet should be doing. Why waste water that can feed your garden?

- **Go organic if it works in your area.**

Organic methods help retain soil moisture and can have a higher yield.

- Harvest, capture and store water.
Rainwater is naturally captured and stored in ponds. Using rainwater for livestock and irrigation is a great way to lessen the impact on local groundwater.

- Retain the moisture of the soil by using compost and mulch. Extreme weather events are causing a definite rise in temperatures in certain parts of the world. By using compost and mulch, you can retain some of the moisture and reduce water evaporation.

- Educate yourself about anything water conservation related. How to rotate crops, how to protect crops, increase yield, grow local indigenous crops, etc.

This includes being knowledgeable about weather systems and patterns.

The water-related problems of the day, affect not just the individual, but the whole community of land owners.
We have to investigate and part of the process is to look at the problem from all angles.

Saving means More

Saving water is very rewarding in the long run. It means that you will put less stress on your water supply and stored water will last longer. Some simple measures to save water and minimize waste:

- When brushing your teeth, turn off the tap. You can save up to 1.5 gal (6L) of water a minute.
- Take shorter showers. You can easily save more than 1.5 gal (6L) a minute. Showers are more water-efficient than bathing.
- Check and double-check all pipes, shower heads and faucets for leaks.
- Replace older toilets, shower-heads and faucets with efficient "water-saving" products.
- Place a water displacement device in your toilet tank. This reduces water usage with every flush.
- Design and implement a grey water system. Shower and washing machine runoff can be reused.
- Create a water-smart garden or no-waste irrigation set-up for crops.
- For small gardens, use a watering can instead of a hose.
- Educate your family about awareness. Wash dishes by hand, don't flush every time, plug the tub when you shower, etc.
- Install a water meter. The evidence of water fees will encourage saving.

Try to calculate your household's water consumption to see where you can save.

CHAPTER 02

Finding a Water Source for Your Land

It's only when we try to find water ourselves, that we realize just how hard it can be. When looking at buying rural land, finding a dependable water source should be your first concern. In looking for water, you have three basic options:
- Public or municipal water is water that's provided by the government in service to the people. Certain rural areas may not be serviced by a municipal water system.
- Surface water includes water from a river, stream, lake, or spring.
- Groundwater is water pumped from a well.
Do not even think about buying a property if your water source is not guaranteed. Don't let emotion get the better of you. Make sure you do your research, for in certain areas potable water is scarce and to make it work, you'll have to become an expert at water management. I'll go so far as to say that, when buying a property, finding water is not an afterthought, it is the decider. Factors like surface

water, groundwater, depth of the water table, local rainfall and community preparedness, all have to be taken into account. You also have to consider the possibility of contamination through runoff from adjacent properties. Living downhill from a farm that uses harmful pesticides means that during a rain event your property will be affected adversely. Areas prone to flooding are more susceptible to pathogen contamination due to stagnant water formation that causes microbe proliferation. This can cause a myriad of problems down the line.

If you want to avoid these issues, you will have to make a thorough assessment of the water situation not only on your land, but also in the surrounding communities. This also applies to current landowners who might be dissatisfied with their water situation, for whatever reason.

Unfortunately, in many areas you will need government approval, in the form of permits and licenses, before you can drill a well, harvest rain from the roof or develop a spring running through your property.

No matter which direction you choose, the first and most obvious step will be to examine the information provided by your local government. You can go downtown to the department of water management or to a water utility office. Alternatively, you can also view the information provided online, by various government agencies. Let's take a look at the different options.

Public Water

Having access to the public water supply is considered a great benefit, since you are almost always guaranteed a steady flow from the faucet. When buying a new property, this kind of information will be provided by the seller, sales agent or on a government provided land listing. It should clearly state whether the land is served by a public water supply line. On paper this sounds wonderful, but the reality is that your water has a long way to travel between source and faucet, which means that many variables can influence the quality of the water before it flows out your kitchen tap. It will be worth your while to investigate the potability of your water and if contaminants are found to be present, to

Before buying

- Investigate extreme weather patterns in the area and the probability of droughts and floods.

- Research regulations concerning rainwater harvesting and having a well.

- Find the expected annual rainfall for the area.

- Talk to neighbors about their experiences.

- Check the depth of the local water table.

- Investigate all surface water souces.

be aware of the options at your disposal. You will have to do some investigation yourself to determine what forms of water sources are available. A property that's within the city limits will definitely have access to a public main water line. This is provided through a network of pipes that's managed by the government or a government appointed entity. Many rural properties are also connected to the public water line. In some areas the water is supplied by a local community well. This is also considered a form of "public water" and similarly you will have to apply for the right to join this well. There are of course properties without public water or community wells. This means that you will have to improvise to find an alternative source of water.

• The Main Water Line

Find out where the main water line is located and where the original source is located. Inquire as to the quality of the source and also about the water pipes and if asbestos cement pipes are still in circulation. You want to avoid contaminants, or at the very least, be aware of them. Concerning connecting to the main water line, make sure that you get comprehensive answers concerning the following:

- *Be legal*

Make sure you know which permits and legal documentation are required to connect to this main water line.

- *Fees*

Spring Water

Springs are usually fed by shallow groundwater. Some springs seep out of banks, slopes or hills and typically groundwater emerges from one defined discharge in the earth's surface. This is called a concentrated spring.

Others "seep" from the ground over a large area and has no defined discharge point. This is a seepage spring.

• Determine if it's year-round water. Look for signs like plant growth with roots growing towards the water source.
Is there a worn-out channel for water to flow, indicating flow over a long period of time? Check the temperature of the water throughout the day. A constant temperature indicates consistent flow; the water should be slightly cooler than the air.

• Take a sample and have it tested.

• Determine the flow rate. Take a pipe and see how long it takes to fill a bucket (E.g. measure 5 gallons/ 19L). Best to do it during the dry season, when the water table is at it lowest.
Springs used for drinking water supplies should yield at least 2 gallons/7.5L per minute throughout the entire year.

• Call an expert to cap your spring, or in an emergency, place a black flexible PVC pipe with a screen filter inside the source and secure and cover it without disrupting the original flow channel.

Store the water in a holding tank.

Check the fees to connect to the main water line. In certain countries the government will connect your water free of charge. Check with the local government office to inquire after fees and whether you need a water meter or not. Water meters are very expensive.

- Regulations
Make sure that you get answers regarding the following:

- What regulations will affect your usage of the water?
- Who should install the connection line?
- Does the installation require government inspection or regulation?

• Local Community Water

In more remote areas it's not uncommon for the local communities to pool their resources together and to create a local water well. These wells are operated and maintained by the community members themselves and are considered a "public" water source for the local area. When inquiring about a local community water source, make sure about the following:

- The water quality
Since no government agencies are involved you have to make sure that the water is 100% potable. Take a sample and have it tested at a government-certified laboratory. If your situation is more urgent, and you need an immediate answer, test the water

yourself with a DIY water test kit. These kits are simple to use and very reliable.

- Life expectancy
How long is the water source (well) expected to produce water? This is not a simple question. Understand that the groundwater is dependent on precipitation. If the community extracts water more rapidly than it can be naturally replenished, then you will end up with a dry well. This is where extreme weather events can destroy communities with unexpected droughts.

- Hidden costs
What are the hidden costs, maintenance, infrastructure, etc. Can you access the water line and how much does it cost? Do you need a water meter (expensive)? What are the local rates.

Alternative Sources

Having a community or government provided water source is obviously a great option. You should still look into finding an alternative water source on your land. If you live in a real remote area, this might be your only option. Using surface water from a spring or lake, or groundwater from a well, are both great options to reduce your water bill and to provide you with water in a time of need. To prospective land owners, this means that you will have to make a thorough assessment of your land.

- *Step 1. Walk your land*

Get a general feel for the vegetation and wildlife present. Try to locate areas with lush vegetation compared to their surroundings. Shallow groundwater can be found by knowing the landscape. Vegetation with water-loving plants, like willows and aspen trees will be an indicator of groundwater at shallow depths. Conditions for large quantities of shallow groundwater are more favorable under valleys than under hills. Areas where water is at the surface in a depression such as springs, seeps, or swamps reflect the presence of groundwater, although not necessarily in large quantities or of usable quality. Make notes of all surface water present or evidence of past. If you find a tiny rivulet or stream flowing on your land, track it back to its source. A spring can be a great source of water. Start celebrating if the source provides a year-round, steady flow of clean water, and if it is located within your property boundaries. Call in an expert to help with capping the spring.

- *Step 2. Talk to the locals*

Finding water and knowing about water is something every landowner is willing to discuss and to offer advice about. Questions you should be asking:

a. How deep is the water table and are there springs in the area?

b. What's the water quality like?

c. Does the ground consist of clay, rock or sand?

d. What's the expected yearly local precipitation and which are the wettest months of the year?

- *Step3. Test for presence of water*

If you are completely on your own, in the boonies, then you need to lower a pipe and look for groundwater yourself. This is why you have to do research first. If the locals provided you with hope that there is groundwater at drill-able depth or if you saw unusual lush growth in one area of your land, then you will have to test. Consult an expert to assist you.

- *Step 4. Secure your water rights*

You have to secure the rights to your land. This means, depending on where you live, a visit to your local water office. Your water rights consist of the right to use, a reasonable quantity of public water, for a certain period of time, as it occurs on your property.

- *Step 5. Research*

Use the Internet, the local library or visit a local government office. You must be aware of the water cycles and of the weather systems that affect precipitation in your area. This will give you a fairly clear indication of what to expect over the coming months. Once you are familiar with a certain area, you can use a system of deduction to figure out what is causing a water scarcity or drought. Lakes are fed through rivers, which run down from the mountains. The mountains depend on rain. It is crucial for any Prepper to know the topography and environment that he or she lives in.

• *Step 6. Talk to a licensed well driller or to a hydrologist*

Get a hydrologist to obtain information on the wells in the target area. The locations, depth to water, amount of water pumped, and types of rocks penetrated by wells also provide information on groundwater. Licensed well drillers will not only inform you about drilling for surface water, but also about how to use submersible pumps to extract water from springs and lakes.

Questions to ask a licensed well driller:

- The cost per depth drilled?
- What local regulations apply to drilled wells?
- What permits are required?
- The probability of finding water and the expected depth?
- The soil conditions in the area. Rock, clay, sand or gravel?
- Once you've struck water, what is the life expectancy of the well?
- How will weather cycles (El Nino/ La Nina) affect the water table and the yield of the well?
- For future scenarios, what could possible contamination causes be?

Your Water Rights

In general, your water right consists of the right to use:

1. a reasonable quantity of public water,
2. for a certain period of time,
3. occurring at a certain place.

Governments enforce legislation that's designed to protect the use and enjoyment of water that travels in streams, rivers, lakes, and ponds, gathers on the surface of the earth, or collects underground. If you have the right to divert water from a river, stream, lake, or spring, you have a surface water right. If you have the right to pump water from your well, then you have a groundwater right.

In areas with an abundance of surface water, these rights are mostly accepted, as insisted by the landowner.

In areas prone to droughts and water shortages, things can get more complicated because of competition, and you will have to apply for a permit before you can utilize the water resource.

When applying for water rights, the office with jurisdiction will consider the following:

- The protection of the environment.
- Preventing waste of precious water resources.
- The fair distribution of water resources.

The main focus is to ensure that the public interest is served. Note that you do not own the water, you just own the rights to the use of it.

CHAPTER 03

Extracting Water From The Ground

For thousands of years, man has been digging into the ground, to look for water. Even today, in many developing countries, digging a well is the only way to have access to a potable water source.

For the modern landowner, having a well means independence. It's basically like striking the jackpot of self-sufficiency, for having access to clean, drinkable water takes care of a multitude of land-related problems. By definition, and according to the Oxford Dictionary, a well is "a shaft sunk into the ground to obtain water."

When we dig a little bit deeper, we see that wells are fed by natural aquifers of water that are found underground. These aquifers are pockets of water that are located under the layers of ground that we walk on. The ground, which consists of layers of sand, clay, gravel and rock, acts as a natural filtration system. Not only does it filter, but it also adds vital minerals and ions to the water as it seeps

through. This is a classic example of the Earth providing and catering to our needs. Once this water has traveled down through all these layers, it accumulates in areas with sand, gravel or rock formations. In theory, the deeper you have to go to reach the water, the cleaner it should be. Note that this deep water can also be contaminated with natural occurring chemicals that seep into the groundwater.
Fortunately, we don't have to go too deep to find water. Professional drill teams often go down to 400-500 feet, but in general, most water is found no deeper than 250 feet down. When we look at domestic drill set-ups, we find that the majority of landowners find their water at less than 50 feet. Most of it is used for irrigation and livestock, but with a bit of luck, you can get quality water from right underneath your feet. This is great news for the self-sufficient homeowner who is willing to try his hand at well drilling or digging.
Having access to a well is something that must be on the minds of all people who want to live close to the land.
The water in the cities is transported from reservoirs, rivers, dams and lakes and it is exposed to various pollutants and contaminants. On top of that, it has to be treated for human consumption and that's where even more chemicals are added.

Whether you're unhappy with your current water quality, or just looking for an independent water source, get moving, for it's time to get yourself a shallow water well.

Shallow Water Well basics

First, realize that this is a fairly ambitious project and that you need to plan your well very carefully. Let's look at the different methods used to extract water from the ground. Remember that both soil type and depth of the water table will determine which option is best for you.

Drilling a well yourself

Suitable water table depth:
Up to 35 feet
Soil: Mostly sand and gravel

This might seem a fairly simple method, but it does involve building and designing a drill from scratch using PVC pipe. The drilling is done by sinking a drill-bit into the ground and creating a hole. As the drill-bit cuts the ground material, the cuttings are flushed out with water pressure. Avoid drilling in rock, but dealing with thin layers of clay in between should be no problem.

Digging your own well

Suitable water table depth:
Up to 25 feet
Soil: Sand, clay and gravel

This method involves simple tools and physically digging till you reach water. Dug wells are mostly found in areas where the water table is known to be located at a shallow depth. Personally, I would not recommend digging deeper than 25 feet. This is a time-consuming and very dangerous excavation technique. Shafts often cave-in and there is also the danger of asphyxia. You will need an expert and helpers to assist you with this job. This is not a recommended method!

Using an auger to dig your well

Suitable water table depth:
Up to 20 feet
Soil: Sand and gravel

An auger is a tool used to cut into the ground and once deep enough, you simply extract it to haul the dirt out. You can add extensions as you move along. Once you reach the water table, you lower a well screen to filter out the sediment. It is a safe and simple method, used in soft soil.

Driving a well point

Suitable water table depth:
Up to 25 feet
Soil: Sand and gravel

This method involves the use of a sledge hammer and driving a well point into the ground. As you go deeper, you add extensions to your drill pipe. The well point has a well screen that filters the water as it enters the well.

Hire a professional

When your water table is located under 50 feet, you can use one, or a combination of the above mentioned methods. If you discover that your water table is deeper, then there is only one option available. Get a local well driller to come over and to give you a quote. Expect it to be fairly expensive. These days people pay around US$4,000-10,000 for a well. You are charged by the foot, so the deeper they go, the higher the costs.

The Soil

You will have to take a good look at the type of soil in your area. The dry area of soil above the water table is called the unsaturated zone. This is an area where the soil particles are filled with air and where water droplets are just passing through on their way down to the water table. Very little water is found in this area. The possibility of digging or drilling through this area depends on the layers of soil present.

Sand. On paper, having fine, white sand sounds like a good type of soil to explore for water, but the fact of the matter is that this kind of sand is just packed too loosely. It will collapse on the well pipe and it will do it often. This makes it an extremely complicated medium to drill through. Coarse, yellow sand with large granules and gravel in between is best. (Finding the odd layer of fine sand is not a problem and you can simply go through it.)

Gravel. Drilling through gravel, or a combination of gravel and sand, is the way to go. These layers are filled with air and are thus easy to "push" around. Gravel is permeable

Water Bearing Layers

Sand. Coarse sand is absolutely perfect for finding water. Normally, this sand will be slightly yellow in color. Water moves easily through this type of sand and when you hit a combination of sand and gravel, it's even better.

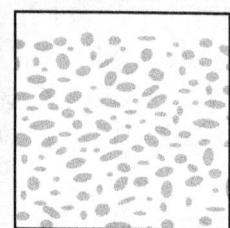

Gravel. Gravel is very much the same as sand in that the air in between the pieces allows the water to flow easily. Gravel is coarse and does not cake together. It is very permeable, just like sand and thus perfect for finding water.

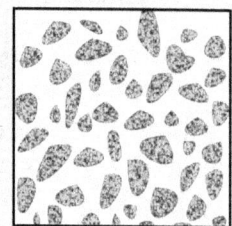

Fractured Rock. Water found in porous rock with fissures can be of very good quality. You will be very lucky to find this type of water. Often you need to drill very deep to reach these rock aquifers and to do this you will need to consult a professional.

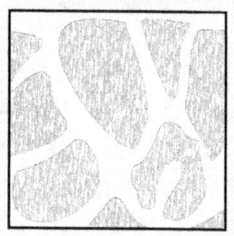

Clay. Clay particles are small. They are also sticky and "cake" together to form solid layers that are impermeable (water can't penetrate). If the soil in your area is know for its clay content don't waste your time. Consult an expert to get a definitive answer.

and good for drilling and finding water.

Clay. Clay particles are tightly packed and do not hold much water. Thick layers of clay is very hard to drill through. Your drill instrument will get stuck in the clay and it can turn into a nightmare very quickly. Drilling or digging through the odd layer of clay is not a problem; it all depends on how much clay is found in your area.

Rock. Finding layers of rock can be a problem. If it's solid and thick rock, you will have to start a new well. If it's a thin layer with broken rock, then you can try to break it up and to remove or to push through it with your drill.

The Water Table

The area just below the water table is called the saturated zone and this is where we find the wet soil. This is where the water comes to rest and where the best quality water is found. All the way at the bottom of the **saturated zone**, we find the bedrock area which is where fractured rock is found with rock aquifers. When drilling or digging your own well you must realize that these are "shallow" wells that we find at the Standing Water Level (SWL). A shallow well will not reach all the way into the rock aquifer. Consider the big picture when thinking about wells and water.

The groundwater is fed through precipitation. Once you have a well up and running, you should take care not to pump it dry. The

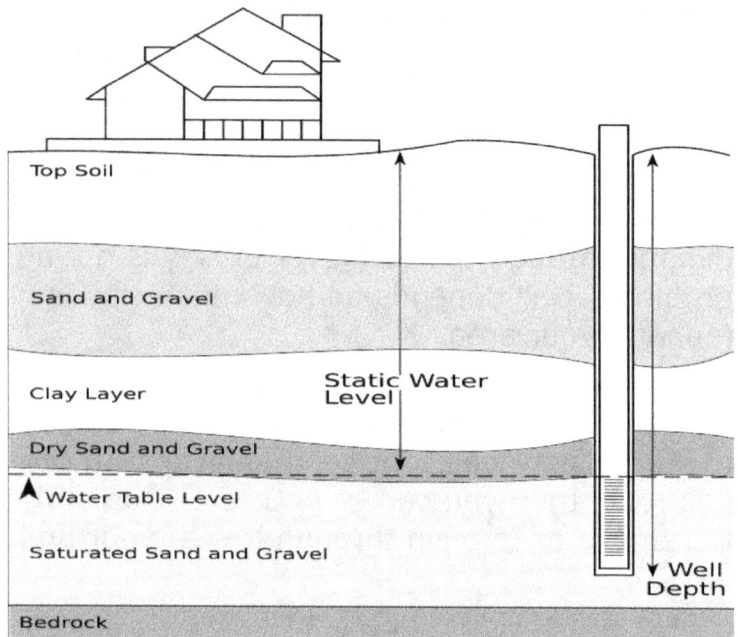

groundwater relies on precipitation during the wet seasons to maintain its level. Pumping your own well dry can possibly affect your neighbor, since you might both be using the same groundwater. This means that you should gather as much info about the local water table as possible and that you are familiar with the local precipitation patterns.

Planning

Step1. Research

- Do your research and read up as much as you can about your local environment. Ask the locals. They know what's been tried and tested in the area. Looking at other wells means that you can get a clear indi-

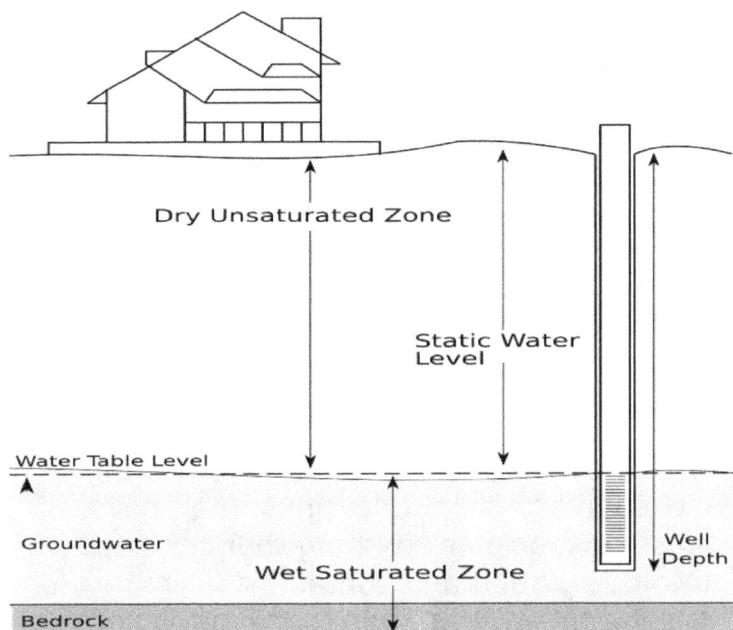

cation how deep the water table lies. Other well owners can also provide valuable information concerning rock and sand formations in your area. Make sure that you know what your land was used for in the past. Contaminants remain in the soil for a long time!

• Look at geological survey records that indicate the location of the local water table. These records are quite informative and they will highlight other wells in the area. Aquifers are also indicated on these surveys and can be found at the same depth as the water table. If the local water table is deeper than 50 feet/ 15m, you will have to ask a professional contractor to drill a well for you.

- Look at topographic maps. They indicate the topography of the land and as a rule of thumb, the lower the elevation, the easier to find water. Look at the slopes in your area and on your property. Will the runoff from rain contaminate your well? Avoid putting a well near a **slope** and look for a flat area with minimum risk of **flooding**.

- In selecting a suitable location, you will have to look at your immediate environment.

a.) Be sensible and avoid areas with enclosed livestock, septic tanks, fuel tanks, waste disposal or anything that can seep into the ground and contaminate your well. A good rule of thumb is to stay uphill of these areas and at least 150 ft/ 50m away. Your local health department will have guidelines concerning this.

b.) Stay at least 30 feet/ 10m from streams and ponds.

c.) In addition, wells should not be located in extremely wet areas with water-logged soil.

- If you have the means, hire a professional consultant. They will do an analysis of the area and provide you with the relevant information.

Step 2. Get Legal

Deal with the local government. In most areas the government requires permits and permissions. Once your well is up and running, you do not want some government representative to come round and rain on your parade. Make sure that all boxes are ticked and that you are legal and complying with local laws.

Step3. Plan the type of well you want

Once you've done your research, established the depth of the local water table and checked with your local government office, you can decide which kind of well will suit you.

Shallow water wells can be drilled yourself where the distance to the water table is no more than 35 feet/ 10.5m. Some home drillers are able to go considerably deeper, but that takes experience and know-how. **A shallow water well can only be used for drinking once it's been tested and deemed safe for human consumption.** Water coming from a shallow water table only traveled a few feet through the soil and it has not been filtered properly. This is information that is not to be ignored. People tend to get excited when they see the clear liquid gushing out of the ground, but keep in mind that there are various natural occurring chemicals in the ground that can affect the quality of your water.

A deep groundwater well must be drilled by a professional. It can easily be 250 feet/ 76m deep and, in theory, the water can be of very good quality (although not always a guarantee).

How To Drill And Construct A Well Using PVC Pipe

Once you've determined the size and location of the local water table, you can consider building a drill. This will be used to drill through the dry, unsaturated zone which consists of multiple layers of soil. We will find water once we reach the wet, saturated zone. This is where we can extract water from the water-bearing sand.

Manual Drilling

Shallow water wells are the only wells that can be drilled manually using a DIY method. Generally speaking, shallow water wells are not considered safe for human consumption. This should not dissuade you from drilling for water. Manual drilling is cheap compared to a machine-drilled well and the water is ideal for irrigation and other domestic applications. Depending on your location, it is possible to find potable water, but that will depend on the quality and depth of the water table.

We will look at a tried and tested method of simple PVC pipe drilling. This method is also called "jetting" of a well. Expect to spend at least of 20-25 hours on this project.

These days you can buy a PVC home drill kit online or at select hardware stores. They include parts, fittings and instructions on how to drill for water. The following setup is based on this method and will give you an idea how to approach basic drilling for water. If you prefer to do things yourself, know that with some basic DIY skills you can build and design your own drill, drill bit and well casing. It is a relatively easy and inexpensive project to take on by yourself. The soil that you are drilling in must be drill-friendly. Soil differs from region to region. As a general rule, expect to drill through layers of top soil, dry sand, clay, rock, water bearing sand and gravel.

You will be aiming to strike water in the layers with sand, gravel or even rock (seldom). Ground with coarse sand and gravel is con-

The use of well water

- Once filtered, it can be used indoors for washing, bathing and cleaning.
- For drinking purposes, you will first have to get your water tested to see if it is actually safe to drink.
- Outdoors it can be used for pools, ponds and recreation.
- Can be used for fire fighting.
- It is perfect for irrigation purposes.
- Good for livestock.
- It is perfect for small scale mining and manufacturing.
- Having a water well means that you don't need to store thousands of gallons of water for an emergency.

sidered best for the DIY driller attempting a shallow water well.

CAUTION. Take note that you will exert yourself physically. It's hard, manual labor, so wear the right clothes and shoes and take a rest when needed. If you have any health issues, you should first check with your doctor.

Let's take a look at the **basics of well drilling** and the different materials that can be used. Note that this is a project that should be started early in the morning. Once you start "drilling" and have water flowing you cannot remove the drill since the inside of the hole will collapse and if you leave it in the hole, the drill pipe will get stuck. Plan carefully and prepare material and equipment in advance. This is preferably a two man job.

When looking at the diagram (p.39) we can see the basic drilling method in action. Water is pushed through a PVC pipe with a drill bit at the bottom. **This pipe initially functions as the drill pipe and later it will be used as the well casing pipe**. The water is forced down the drill pipe to soften the ground at the bottom, and as the drill tip cuts away at the soil, the water flushes all the cuttings up to the top along the outside of the drill pipe. The action is flush, cut, flush and it is repeated continuously. This PVC pipe will also prevent the ground, surrounding it, from caving in and therefore we can also call it the well casing. Once the hole is deep enough and you've reached the water table, you can insert a well screen all the way to the bottom of the well. A well screen consists of two parts. The longest part consists of pieces of PVC pipe glued together with inside PVC slip couplings (long). At the end of this PVC pipe you connect the well screen that is 4-6 feet long. A well screen can filter the sand particles and allow the water to enter the well pipe. This complete well screen is just as long as your well casing. Once the well screen is in place, you can slowly pull the well casing pipe up to expose the slits of the screen. You want the water bearing sand to collapse around the well screen, because that is where the water will enter your well. You now have two options. You can leave the well casing in place, to maintain the structure of the well. You can also remove it completely, but then you'll have to fill the open area around the well pipe with sand and gravel. You can add a hand pump or electrical

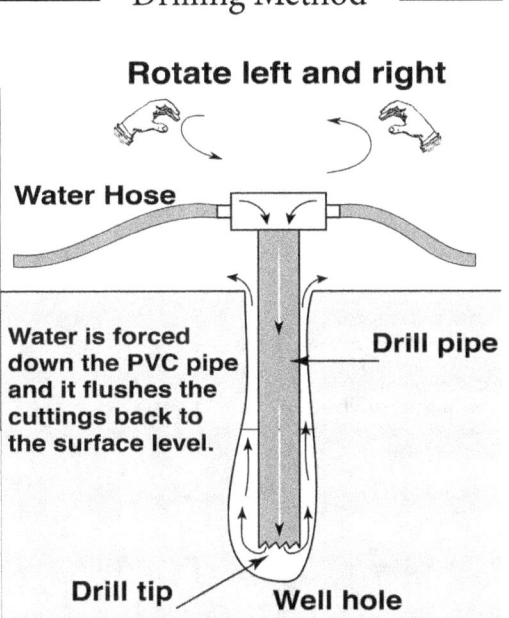

Drilling Method

Rotate left and right

Water Hose

Water is forced down the PVC pipe and it flushes the cuttings back to the surface level.

Drill pipe

Drill tip

Well hole

Extracting Water From The Ground

Well Drilling Basics

1. Start the hole by rotating the drill left and right. Allow the water to flow and to saturate the soil.

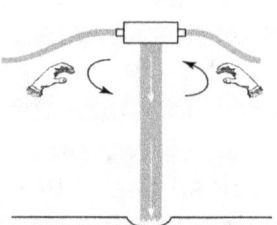

The water, flowing from the two hose pipes, is softening the ground and flushing the cuttings to the surface level.

2. Drill down through all the layers of soil till you reach the water table. Add PVC pipe (with couplings) as you go deeper.

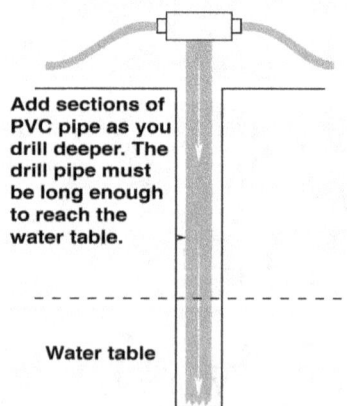

Add sections of PVC pipe as you drill deeper. The drill pipe must be long enough to reach the water table.

Water table

3. Remove the drill top and leave the drill pipe inside the hole. This pipe now acts as the well casing.

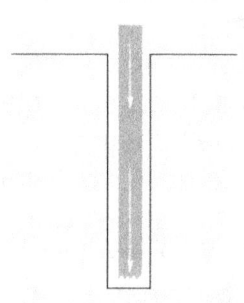

4. Prepare your well screen by adding sections of PVC pipe (or to cut one long piece) till it's just as long as the well casing.

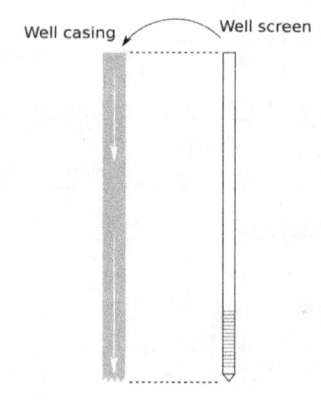

Well casing   Well screen

Extracting Water From The Ground

Well Drilling Basics

5. Slide the well screen into the well casing. The well screen should reach inside the water-bearing sand at the bottom.

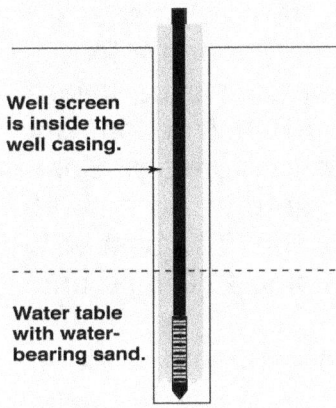

6. Pull the well casing up till it's above the well screen. This is a simple method to expose the slits in the well screen to the water-bearing sand.

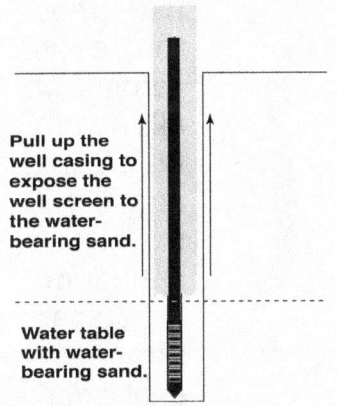

7. Pour pea gravel down the side of the well casing. It should cover the length of the well screen.

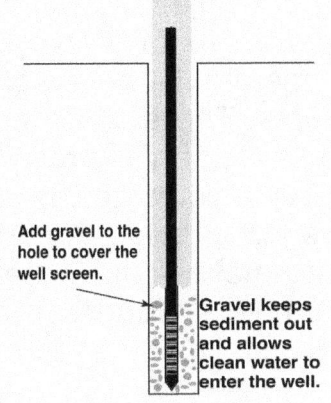

8. Leave the well casing in place; this is your well. You can also pull out the well casing and fill the annular space around the well pipe with sand.

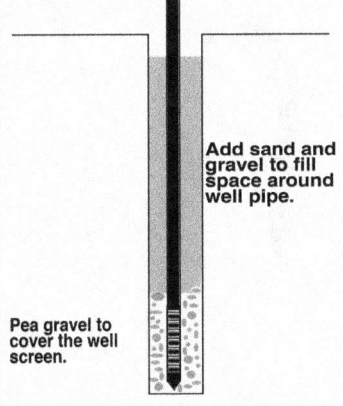

Extracting Water From The Ground

pump to extract water from your well.

Construct Your Drill

Step 1. The Drill Top

Before you can drill into the ground to make a bore-hole, you will need to construct a "drill". You have an option of buying a PVC home drill kit online or from select hardware stores. These kits come with instructions and the assembly is pretty straightforward. Some provide you with the complete setup and others just provide the drill T-top. The best option is to make your own, by using PVC pipe and plumber's fittings.

Let's start at the top of the drill and work our way down. This section requires some knowledge of joining plumber's fittings. Remember to use PVC cement on all joints. Be creative and adapt to your situation. If you cannot find the exact part

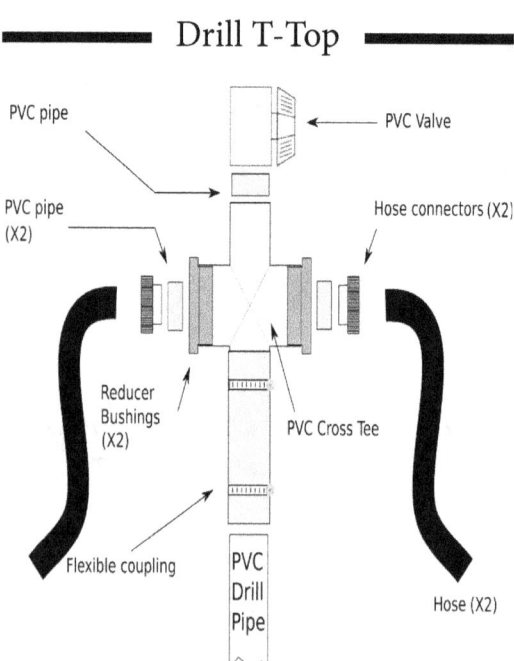

Extracting Water From The Ground

To construct a drill, you'll need the following:

- **PVC cement and primer.** To join all fittings and PVC pipes.
- **Hosepipes x 2.** To flush the hole and to push the cuttings to the top.
- **PVC Cross tee x 1.** This is where water, flowing from the two hoses, are redirected into the main drill pipe. (2" recommended)
- **PVC valve x 1.** The PVC valve allows for air and water (under pressure)to be released from the drill. Also adds the option of connecting a mud pump. (2" recommended)
- **PVC pipe pieces x 2.** To connect hose connectors to reducer bushings. ($3/4$" recommended)
- **PVC reducer bushing x 2.** These connect the hose connectors to the PVC Cross tee. (2" reduced to $3/4$" recommended)
- **Hose connectors x 2.** They connect the reducer bushings to the hose pipes. ($3/4$" recommended)
- **Flexible coupling x 1.** Rubber tubing with radiator clamps will also do. (2" recommended)
- **PVC pipe piece x 1.** Connects to the bottom of the PVC Cross tee. See next page. (2" diameter and 5" long recommended)
- **Drill pipe handle bar.** Made of wood. It allows you to control the drill.
- **PVC drill pipes 8-10 feet in length.** With bell- or plain ends.
Once joined, they will be the drill pipe and well casing. (2" recommended)
- **PVC well pipes.** They connect to the well screen. Your well pipe can be one long pipe, or sections joined together.
This pipe will be connected to your well screen. ($1^{1/4}$" recommended)
- **Well screen.** This is where the water enters the well.
- **PVC Couplings.** These connect the long drill pipes and the well pipes. Use outer couplings for the drill pipes and inner couplings for the well pipes. (2" recommended)
- **Pump.** Once finished, you will need a pump to extract the water from the well. The pump connects to the top of the well pipe.

The Drill

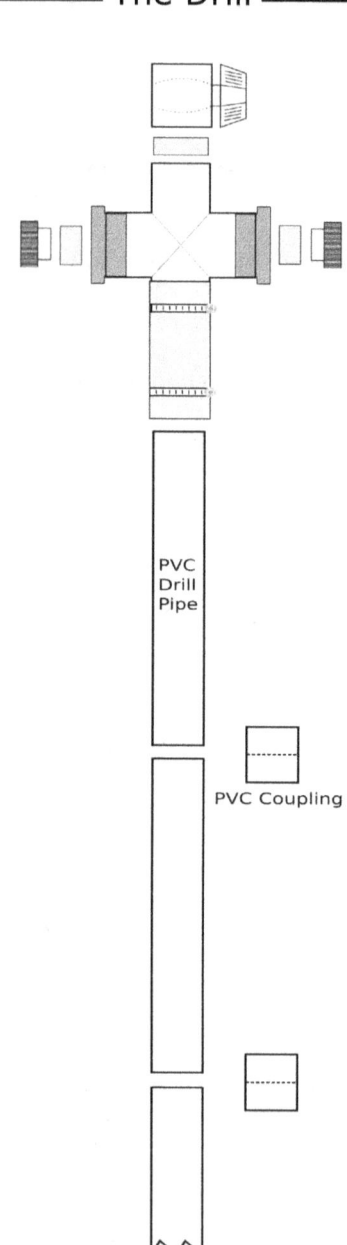

or fitting, then you have to improvise. Remember to use Schedule 40 PVC pipe; you can use 2", 3" or even 4" PVC pipe. The larger the diameter, the more flushing power you will require from the hose pipes.

Starting with 2" is a good safe size for your first attempt at drilling. If your drill pipe is 2" you can adjust all fittings to accommodate this size. Make sure that the water from the hoses flow freely and without obstruction. You need as much flushing power possible. Before you start, make sure you look at all the material you will need on page 43.

Breakdown of the T-Top upper part of the drill.

- **The PVC Cross**

Extracting Water From The Ground

Tee acts as the main facilitator that allows water into the drill pipe. The bottom of the Cross Tee connects with the drill pipe. If your drill pipe is 2", then use a similar sized cross tee of 2". Remember that as you drill deeper, you will have to remove the drill-top to add more pipe to the drill. This means that the design must be practical enough to allow the top to be removed and replaced.

The top of the Cross tee connects to the PVC valve. The two sides of the Cross tee connect to the reducer bushings and then to the two hose pipes.

- **The PVC Valve** that goes into the top part of the Cross tee allows you to release air or water from the chamber when needed. You can also connect it to a pump at a later stage. It is a handy option to have. Depending on the fittings you use (threaded or not), you might need a piece of PVC pipe to join the valve and the Cross tee.

- **Reducer bushings** (x2) are used to reduce the size of the PVC Cross tee down to the size of the hose connectors.

- **Hose connectors** (x 2) will allow water to flow from the hose pipes through your reducer bushings. Make sure they fit your hosepipe connectors before you buy. To join the hose connectors to the reducer bushings, you will need two short pieces of $^3/_4$" PVC pipe.

The Flexible Coupling

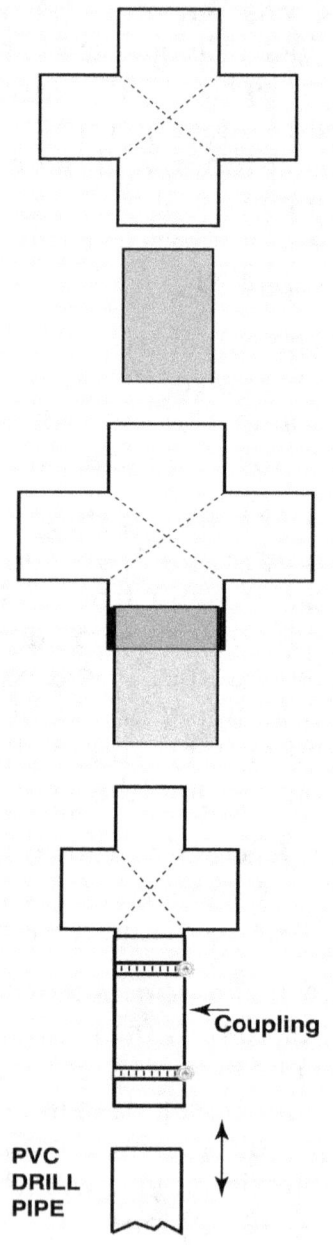

1. The Cross Tee is to be joined to the piece of PVC (grey color). Line the 2 pieces up and add PVC cement and primer. This combined unit forms the top of the drill that will connect to the drill pipe.

2. Join the 2 pieces. Later the other end of the PVC pipe will slide into your drill pipe. No cement needed there, because you have multiple pieces of drill pipe to add later.

3. The flexible coupling joins the drill top and drill pipe. To change drill pipes, loosen the bottom screw of the flexible coupling and add a new pipe section.

PVC DRILL PIPE

Extracting Water From The Ground

• **Hose pipes** (x 2) that will comfortably reach your drill hole location and at least 15 feet of extra clearing for when the drill pipe is raised. Check the water pressure from faucets. You might have to consult a neighbor to lend you a hose with water pressure coming from his side. The combined water pressure will be great for flushing the hole. The hose pipes connect with the hose connectors.

• **Flexible coupling** (x 1). If you cannot find a flexible coupling, you can improvise with some rubber tubing and radiator clamps. This coupling connects the drill head to the drill pipe. As you drill deeper, you will reach the end of the first drill pipe's length. This means that you have to remove the drill head from the drill pipe. The next step is to connect another drill pipe to the one in the hole. After you have connected the drill pipe in the hole to the new one, you will reconnect the drill T-top to the top of the new pipe. The flexible coupling will allow you to do all of this.

• **PVC pipe** (x 1) cut 5" long. Your drill pipe and your PVC Cross tee are both the same diameter. To join them together, you will use this section.

• **Use PVC cement** with PVC cement primer to join the fittings. Look for a brand that sets within a fairly short period of time. (Later you will use the PVC cement to add drill pipe during the drilling process.)

Make sure that when you assemble the parts (before using the PVC cement), that they all fit snuggly and that there are no loose air gaps. You can get creative with the design of your drill T-top. When picking up your plumber's fittings know that you can tweak the design as you like, but leave ample space for water to flow unobstructed and smoothly through the fittings. If you find that some of your fittings do not have a threaded end, then join them with PVC pipe and cement.

Step 2. The Drill Pipes

The combined length of drill pipes must be long enough to penetrate into the water table. Typically, the drill pipe is made from 8-10 feet sections of 2 inch PVC pipe. The wider the pipe the stronger the flushing power required to flush the cuttings. You can use standard PVC pipes or the ones with the bell endings (which means you can join them without couplings).

To join the drill pipes you will need:

- PVC cement with primer.
- Long outer couplings to join pipes together.
- 2" PVC drill pipes cut to 8-10 feet in length. The combined length of these pipes should reach into the water table.

Calculate the maximum depth you are willing to go by looking at the local water table in your area. You will need at least 3 or 4 pieces of pipe.

Draw lines, measured in feet, on every pipe to indicate the drilling depth.
You can add a setting screw on every coupling if you feel all the twisting and turning might loosen the pipes.

Step 3. The Drill Bit

The drill bit is the part that breaks up the dirt at the bottom of the hole. It scrapes the dirt away, breaks it up and then the water flushes it to the top of the hole. To make your drill bit you have three options.

• The first option is to simply cut teeth into the lead PVC drill pipe. Serrated edges are best and you can manage this with an electric grinder or manually with a hacksaw. You can use this option for soft shallow drilling, but it is not a recommended option since the teeth will wear down easily.

• The second option is to make a replaceable bit from a PVC coupling. Just connect the coupling with PVC cement and once dry use a saw to cut the triangular teeth for the drill bit. This can be an effective drill bit in soft soil, but as you go deeper the teeth will undoubtedly wear out.

• The third option is the best option. Get a piece of galvanized plumbing pipe. Serrated edges are best and you can manage this with an electric grinder or manually with a hacksaw. This drill bit will allow you to cut more effectively through sediment, roots and debris. You can add a short screw to set this drill bit in place since the constant turning of the drill pipe will loosen the drill bit.

Step 4. The Drill Handle Bar

You can make a handle for your drill from wood. A piece of wood fastened with hose clamps will work just fine.

Remember that this handle must be moved up the drill as you add your PVC drill pipe extensions. The hose clamps are easy to unscrew and when adding pipe, it will allow you to place the handle around the new piece of PVC drill pipe.

Preparations

Before you start drilling, lay out the individual pieces and make sure all equipment and tools are ready. Check that hoses are the correct length, fitted with correct connections, and will provide enough water pressure. Double-check your T-top and make sure you have a screwdriver ready for later when needed to loosen the hose clamps.

Your drill pipes should be 8-10 feet long with lines drawn to indicate drilling depth and a mark where you will refasten the grip handle. This saves time for when you have to add pipe and reposition the grip handle.

If you are connecting your pipes with couplings, then a coupling should be fitted to each extra length of pipe beforehand. When dealing with pipes this long, you need strong couplings with long connections.

Get a crate or platform to stand on to make

things easier. A ladder is not a stable platform. Do not stand on a ladder when drilling.

How To

When everything is ready, you can start to drill. You should know your water table depth, to give you an indication as to how deep to drill. You do need a fair amount of luck on your side to hit the water table with your first try. Make sure that you have a helper since drilling is very hard to do on your own.

Be prepared to dig quite a few holes. Do not prepare the well drilling site by digging any large diameter holes beforehand. Remember that water will be flushed out of the hole for an extended period of time and if not careful you'll soon be standing in a lake of water. Just focus on the hole made by the drill head in front of you and make sure water can drain away from the hole.

1. Start the hole

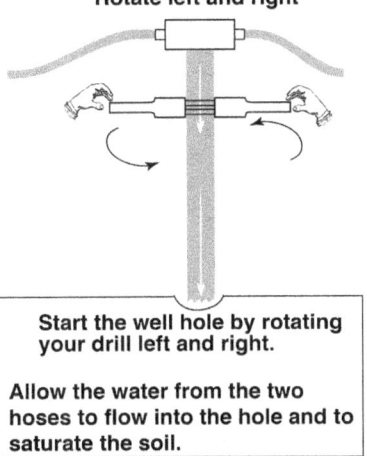

Start the well hole by rotating your drill left and right.

Allow the water from the two hoses to flow into the hole and to saturate the soil.

This is physical, hard labor. You must be in good shape and fairly fit. To start the hole, put your drill pipe down and start twisting it side to side.
Turn the water on slowly. Leave the top valve of the drill

Extracting Water From The Ground

head slightly open, just enough for air pressure buildup to escape. Rock the pipe side to side and twist it sideways with the aim of making the hole wider. Ensure an ample flow of water.

2. Drill deeper

Once you've progressed to about two feet down, you can start to move the drill up and down to flush the hole with water. This is very important. This action, combined with water flow, is essential to keep the pipe from getting stuck.

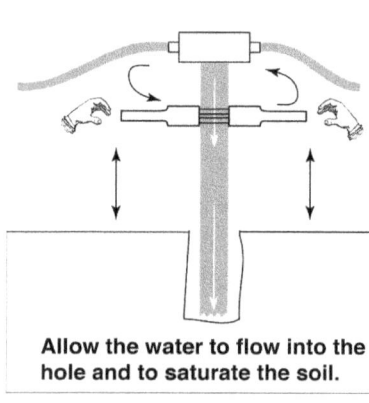

Allow the water to flow into the hole and to saturate the soil.

Constantly keep your eyes on the water coming from the hole. Look for the cuttings and pay attention to the color of the water. Be patient. Do not rush anything. You will be drilling for a few hours, so settle in and commit to the task at hand.

3. Add extra pipe

Add more lengths of PVC pipe as you move along. You should have the pipes prepared (with their couplings if necessary) beforehand. This is where a second person will come in very handy. Try to change pipes as quickly as possible. You do not want to stop the flow of water down the well. The whole process should look like this:

1. Turn off the water.
2. Take off the T-top.
3. Take off the handle grip and fit it to the new pipe.
4. Apply PVC primer and cement.
5. Connect the new pipe.
6. Reattach the T-top and turn on the water.

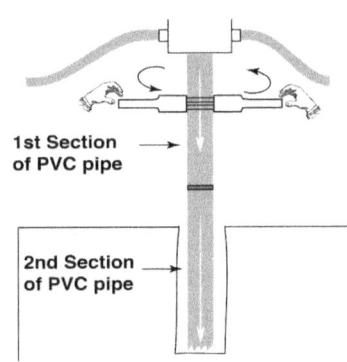

Make sure that the new connection is secure and that the PVC cement is dry. You can add a short screw to every coupling if you feel the need.

4. Add more pipe

Continue drilling and add more lengths of pipe as you go deeper.
When you hit a depth of 10 feet, slow down and make sure that the water is flowing steadily. You should pay extra attention to the up and down movement of the drill. This is where the ground becomes harder and you want to make sure you don't get your pipe stuck. Be patient and proceed slowly while making sure the ground stays saturat-

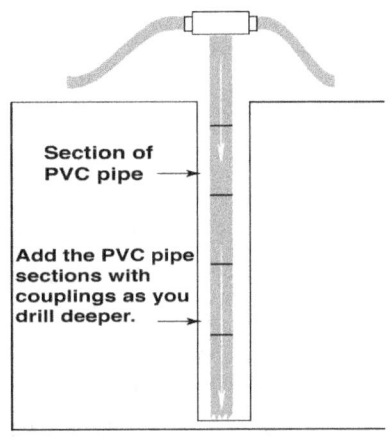

ed with water.

5. How will you know when you've hit water?

It's not easy to tell when you've hit water. The cuttings and water are constantly flowing out of the hole and this can create confusion. Look for sand. Water bearing sand is coarse and light in color. You will recognize this sand when you see it. Don't stop. Let it flow and go a few feet deeper till you find the coarser sand. Expect to find it at the water table depth that you have researched for your area.
Let go of the handle and watch your drill "settle" in the hole. It should sink deeper onto the hole all on its own, indicating that you have reached the water table.

6. Drill deeper

Continue to drill deeper. You want your well to penetrate nice and deep into the water table and to be surrounded by the coarse, yellow sand.
Work that drill up and down and side to side and try to make the hole as big as possible. Your drill pipe should feel very loose inside the hole. Go as deep as you can while still in the coarse, yellow sand. If you can still go 8-10 feet deeper, then do so.
You should try to be well under the Standing Water Level (SWL) as used by professional drillers. The SWL refers to the level of the water in a well, in a normal rest position when undisturbed and under no-pumping conditions. Once you start pumping the water from

the top, the water level will drop. When you turn off the pump, the water will return to the SWL level. Your well screen top should be 8-10 feet under the SWL.

7. The well screen

A well screen is 4-6 feet long, has a pointy tip and hundreds of tiny slits all along the side. These slits keep the sand out and allow the water to flow into your well. This is the point of entry, where water enters your well.

You can buy your well screen from certain hardware stores or from an online merchant.
Your actual well pipe (that you will stick inside the well casing pipe) can be prepared in advance.

If you are using sections of $1^1/_4$" well pipe (instead of one long well pipe), then join them together with long inside couplings. This will prevent the pipe from getting stuck inside the 2" well casing. This well pipe connects to the well screen. If you used a 2" well pipe to drill with, then your well consists of a piece (or pieces) of $1^1/_4$" PVC pipe with a $1^1/_4$" well screen connected at the bottom. The total length of your well pipe should be approximately just as

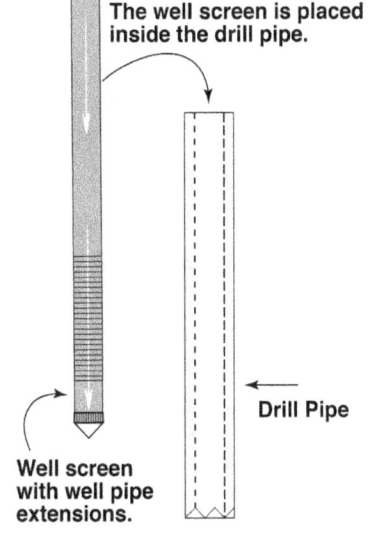

The well screen is placed inside the drill pipe.

Well screen with well pipe extensions.

Drill Pipe

Extracting Water From The Ground

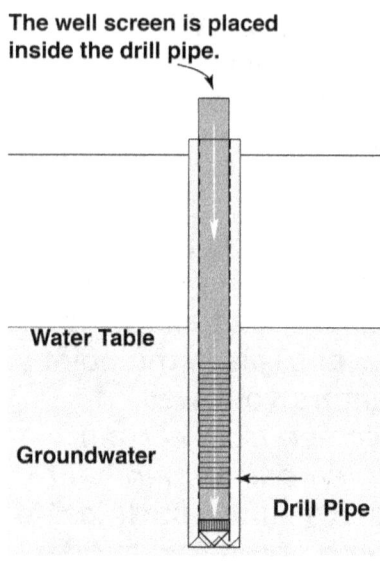

long as the well casing pipe.

Once you've joined the well screen and the well pipe, your well is almost done. At this stage the water is still running. When ready, turn off the water and take off the T-top. Slide your well pipe with the well screen attached all the way down the well casing pipe.

Make sure it has reached the bottom. If your well pipe is the same length as your well casing pipe, then just a small section of well pipe should stick out the top.

Now comes the pullback of the well casing pipe. You have two options.

a.) You can pull the total length of well casing pipe from the hole and then fill the space around your well pipe with sand and gravel. The sand and gravel will allow the water to pass through, but it is coarse enough not to clog your well screen.

Add a concrete apron at the top to keep debris out.

b.) An easier and better option is to pull it up just far enough for the total length of well screen to be exposed to the water-bearing sand.

It will feel strange to pull your well casing back up the hole, but it has to be done. If you leave it in place, you will not get any water from the well. Make sure you are not pulling the well pipe up as well. That's why we suggested inside couplings to be used on the well pipe, so as to not obstruct the well casing pipe when removed.

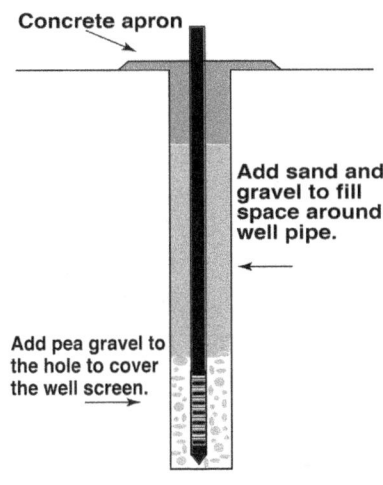

The well screen should be surrounded by coarse sand. Hopefully the sand has completely covered the well screen. If not sure, you can still pour some sand down the hole.

Sand is what you want. It is coarse and prevents plenty of space for water to flow in between and it won't enter your well screen.

Pour some cement all around the top of the well to prevent debris and runoff to contaminate your well.

Cut the well casing

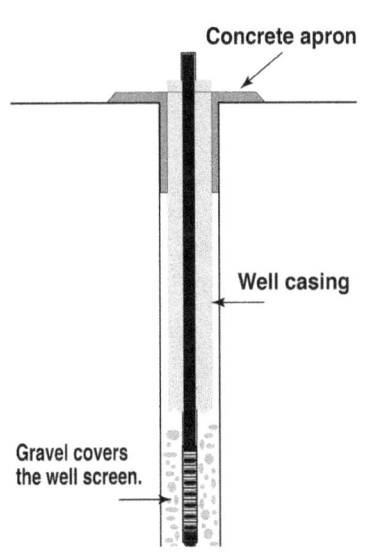

Extracting Water From The Ground

pipe (that's sticking out the top) shorter.

8. The Pump

Install a hand-pump at the top of your well. Use this pump to develop the well and to remove the sediment from the bottom. This could take a while.
Remember that off-the-shelf hand-pumps are mostly used for depths up to 20-25 feet. These pumps have to be primed to get the water from 20 feet down all the way up into the pump.
If you cannot or don't want to prime your pump, then you will need to install a check valve. It is a one-way valve that allows water to go up towards the pump, but not down and

When your pipe gets stuck

1. One option is to use a mechanical instrument like a winch or a hydrolic jack.

2. Try designing a lever with a long handle that rests on a fulcrum.

Move the fulcrum as close possible to the pipe. The lever should push up against the drill pipe handle, which should be reinforced with extra clamps.

3. As a last resort, you can try to sink a smaller diameter pipe ($1/2$ or $3/4$ inch) right alongside your drill pipe to get the soil liquefied again and to loosen it.

out. Having a check valve means that you don't constantly have to prime the hand pump.

The result is that you always have water at the ready in the pump.

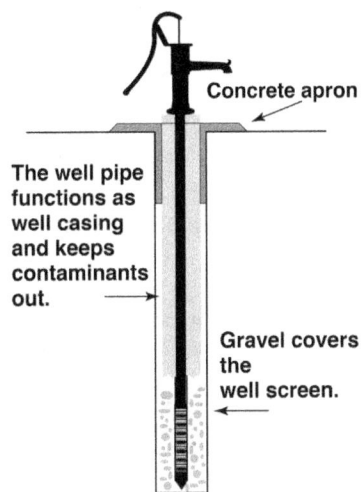

If you are close to an electrical source then you have an option of installing a simple jet pump.

Conclusion

When drilling for water, just keep in mind that you are extracting water from the water table. Keep things simple as possible and remember to focus on longevity. You want the whole structure to last for as long as possible and therefore you have to use quality material (Schedule 40 PVC) and make sure that all fittings are sealed and tight. Examine the process of drilling and see if your own expertise will allow you to come up with an even better solution. Safety should always be a priority and do not take any short cuts. Keep animals and people (children) away from the area. Fill, cover and seal the well opening if you decide to abandon it.

If you have any health issues, you should first check with your doctor before starting this project.

How to pour pea gravel around the well screen?

• The drill pipe is a 2 inch PVC pipe and once the well is finished, it becomes the well casing.

• The well pipe is the 1¼ inch PVC pipe that we connect the well screen to.

• Eventually, the well pipe is placed inside the drill pipe (well casing).

1. If you are using 2" drill pipe, drill down to the desired depth.
Example: 25 feet.

2. Move your drill pipe from side to side, up and down, to widen the hole.
The bottom of the hole should be considerably wider than your 2" drill pipe.
Having a wider bottom space means that we can fill it with plenty of pea gravel.

3. Prepare your 1¼ inch well pipe, with well screen, in advance.
Remember that both your well pipe, and drill pipe, should be more or less the same length (in this case, 25 feet).
When you add the 3 foot long well screen, the well pipe will be around 28 feet long.
The 28 foot long well pipe, all glued together, will later be placed inside the drill pipe.

4. Once you feel that the bottom of the hole is wide enough, you can stop the water and remove the T-top. We are working with a 3 foot long well screen, so take some pea gravel and pour 3 feet of gravel down the drill pipe. As you pour the gravel, work the pipe up and down. The gravel will fill the space underneath the pipe and gradually, as you pour, the pipe will move up. When your drill pipe is three feet higher than it was, it means that you have three feet of gravel inside your hole.

5. This is where the pointed tip of the well screen comes in handy. Slide the whole 1¼ inch well pipe down the 2 inch drill pipe. The well screen will hit bottom (the gravel). Both pipes will be at the same depth in the well. Start to turn and twist the well point and try to work it deeper into the gravel layer. The pointed tip will help in getting it through the pieces of gravel. It will take some time, but you will manage.

6. Once the 28 foot long well pipe and the 25 foot long drill pipe are sticking out at the same level, then you can stop. This means that you have three feet of well screen exposed to the pea gravel at the bottom of your well.

(For a 3" drill pipe, first slide the 1¼" well pipe down inside. Pour the pea gravel down the annular space between the 3" and 1¼" inch pipes. Unlike a 2" pipe, the space between a 3" and 1¼" pipe is enough.)

How To Dig And Construct A Well Using An Auger

In suitable soil conditions, using an auger can be a straightforward method for water extraction. You "scoop" out the soil till you reach the water table. Place a well screen in the hole and use a pump to extract your water.

Auger Drilling

Another very simple method to extract water is to use an auger post-hole digger for drilling.
Augers can be used in sand and gravel or a combination of both. You'll have less success in clay and absolutely no success in rock.
A 6-8 inch auger should be enough. This is basically a fancy drill bit with a handle and it slowly bores into the ground as you turn it. A T-handle will give you more leverage and grip, especially when you get past 10 feet.
Once the auger is filled with dirt, you have to lift it out of the hole and empty it out.
You can add extension rods to the auger as you go deeper. This method is obviously useful for digging shallow wells with appropriate soil conditions.
With an auger, expect to drill to a maximum

You will need:

- An Auger, post-hole digger.
- Metal extension rods (20-25 feet).
- PVC pipe.
- A PVC well screen.
- PVC cement and primer.
- A length of rope and PVC bailer.
- A pump to bail water.
- A hacksaw.

depth of around 20 feet. It will be a slow and energy sapping process. Once you have reached the desired depth, you can fit a PVC well screen inside the hole. The well screen allows clean water to enter your well.

Seal your well and add a hand-pump or centrifugal pump.

How To

1. Get started. Put the auger in the ground. Start drilling by turning the auger in a clockwise direction.

This will ensure that you are drilling straight down.
Do this throughout the process of drilling.

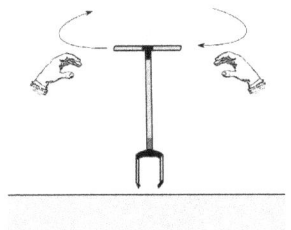

Take your time and be patient. This is time-consuming and hard work.

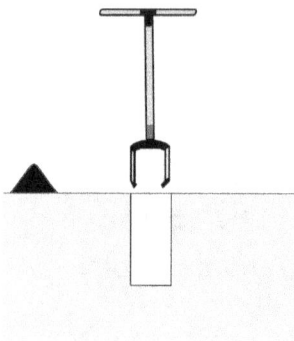

2. Soil. When full, pull it up and empty it. Repeat.
Go as deep as the auger will allow you. Keep the extracted dirt in a heap nearby. You can use it later to seal your well.

3. Extensions. Add extensions when necessary. Make sure that they are tightened securely. Be patient. It will become harder and harder to turn the auger. Get a second person to assist. As you go deeper and deeper, keep an eye on the depth that you have drilled. Once you bring up more water than dirt, you've hit the water table. You should know the depth of the water table in your area beforehand.

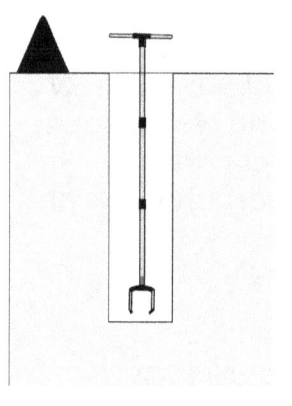

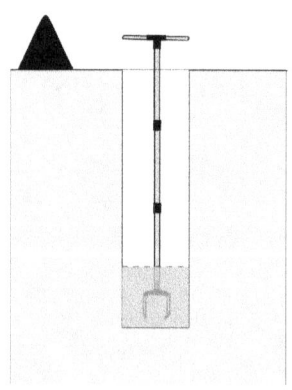

4. Water table. Once you reach the water table, you still have to go deeper.
Don't get over-excited. You need to be nice

and deep inside the water table to have a working well with steady water flow. Measure the depth and aim to go at least another 8 feet deeper.

5. Water. Bail the well when water seeps in. You can try to do it manually, but it's always more effective to use a pump.
If you do it manually, you will need a PVC bailer tied to a rope. (See p.70)

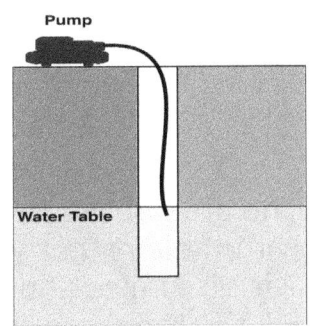

6. Well screen. Well screens are used for sand or gravel aquifers where we want to prevent particles from entering the well. Once connected, it functions as part of the well pipe and it works like a sieve that extends into the water table and that lets the water into the well pipe while filtering out sand and debris.

You can buy a well screen online or make your own from PVC pipe. (See page 68.) For a standard well dug with an 8" auger you can use a 4-6" well screen casing. Cap the bottom of you well casing pipe with

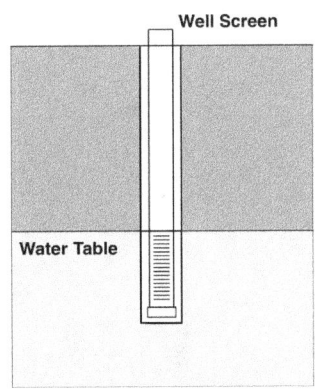

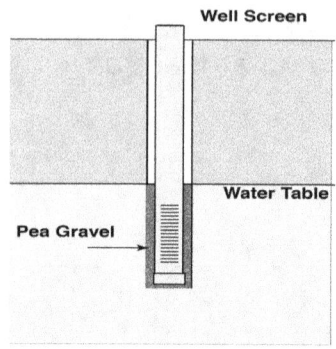

PVC primer and PVC cement. Make sure it's a perfect seal, nice and tight.
Fill the annular space around the well screen with pea gravel.
This will help to keep sediment and silt from clogging the well screen slits.
The area above the well screen can be filled with the dirt that you excavated earlier. Pack it in nice and tight.
Fill the top three feet with concrete and make a nice apron all around your well.

7. Pump. Install a hand-pump at the top of your well, about 3 feet above ground level (to protect from flooding).
Remember that off-the-shelf hand-pumps are mostly used for depths up to 20-25 feet. These pumps have to be primed to get the water from 20 feet down all the way up into the pump. Not priming the pump will cause damage to the leather cup inside.

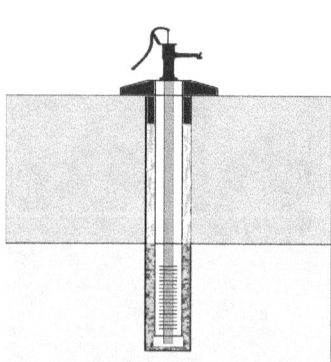

If your water is deeper than 8' down, consider installing a foot valve. This is an inlet valve, connected to the well pipe, that is positioned

about 6" from the bottom of the well. It is a one-way valve that allows water to go up to the pump, but not down and out.
Having a foot valve means that u don't constantly have to prime the hand pump, since the line is filled and you have water at the ready in the pump.

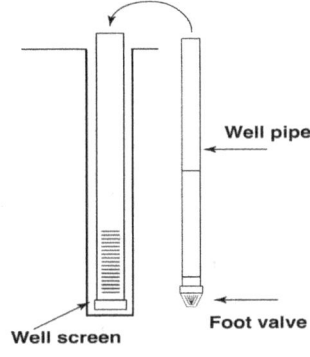

CAUTION! Note that in cold weather, the water in the pipe will freeze and expand and it can split your pipe or foot valve.

Consider removing the pump or foot valve in freezing temperatures, or draining the pump and suction line.
For deeper wells, a deep well hand pump will work.

If close to an electrical source consider installing a jet pump. See the section on pumps on page 101.

If you have any health issues, you should first check with your doctor before starting this project.

How to make a well screen

The well screen will be used to keep particles and debris out of your well water. It is constructed from PVC pipe and should be an inch or two in diameter smaller than the well hole. **This PVC well screen pipe will also function as the well casing.**
For a 6-8 inch hole, use a 4 inch pipe as your well screen and remember that once you are done, to fill the annular space, around the well screen pipe, with pea gravel.
Make the well screen length 4-6 feet long. This means that you should be at least 8-12 feet into your water table. The deeper you can go the better.
You will need a hacksaw to saw slits into the PVC pipe. Use a new, thin blade. You can choose how you want to group the slits together. The main thing is not to compromise the structural integrity of the pipe, by placing the rows of slits too close to one another. For a large diameter pipe, use a grouping of four lines of slits around the length of the pipe. For a thinner pipe, you can use a grouping of three. You can space them out evenly all along the length of the pipe. You can also experiment with your own design.

CAUTION!
Use common sense when making the slits. Their function is to keep debris and small particles out and they should be positioned and grouped to do just that.
Do not cut through the pipe!
Don't group your slits too close together!

Material needed:

- PVC pipe, as required
- PVC cement and primer
- Hacksaw with new, thin blade
- Measuring tape
- Calculator
- Permanent marker

1. Cap the bottom of the pipe. Use PVC cement and primer and make sure it's a secure fit.

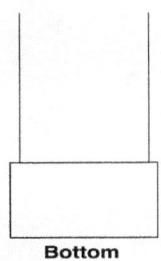
Bottom

5. If you have the patience for it, you can cut a continuous line of slits all along the length of the pipe.

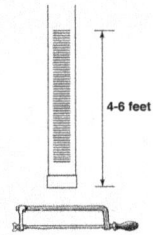
4-6 feet

2. Start the well screen around 4-6" (10-15cm) from the bottom of the pipe. Mark the slits (marker).

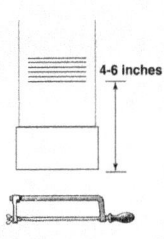
4-6 inches

6. For smaller diameter pipes, cut 3 sections of slits all around the pipe.

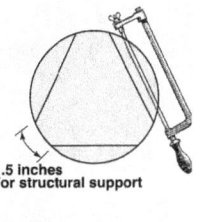
1.5 inches
For structural support

3. Cut the slits into the pipe with a hacksaw. You can group them together in short sections with 3-4 slits.

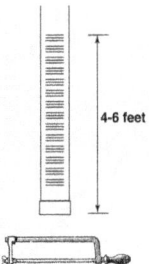
4-6 feet

7. For larger diameter pipes, you can try to get 4 sections of slits in.

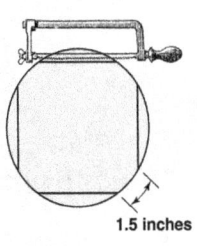
1.5 inches

4. You can also space them out into longer sections with 9 or 10 slits each.

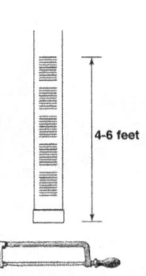
4-6 feet

8. For calculating the length of the slits, you need the circumference of the pipe.

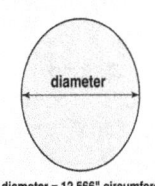
diameter

4" diameter = 12.566" circumference
5" diameter = 15.708" circumference
6" diameter = 18.850" circumference
7" diameter = 21.991" circumference
8" diameter = 25.133" circumference

Extracting Water From The Ground

How to make a PVC bail bucket:

Mechanics:

You will need a long cylindrical bucket, with an opening at the bottom. It should be able to fit inside your well hole.

A simple ball check-valve assembly allows the water to flow into the pipe; when full the ball seats against the reducer and seals it.

Material:

• *Hacksaw*

• *A PVC pipe (2-3 feet) to fit inside the well hole.*

A 4" diameter pipe should fit most holes. This is your bucket.

• *A PVC pipe coupling that will be glued to the bottom of the bucket.*

• *A reducer bushing (4" x 2").*

• *A solid rubber ball that seats against the reducer.*

• *A stainless steel bolt.*

• *PVC cement and primer.*

• *A rope long enough to reach the bottom of the well.*

Directions:

1. Cut your PVC pipe the desired length.

2. Use the PVC cement to attach the coupling to the bottom of the PVC pipe.

3. Glue the reducer bushing to the bottom of the coupling.
The ball seats against the reducer opening.

4. Drill two holes about 6" from the bottom and put the stainless steel bolt through. This prevents the ball from going all the way up.

5. Attach the rope to the top for hauling water.

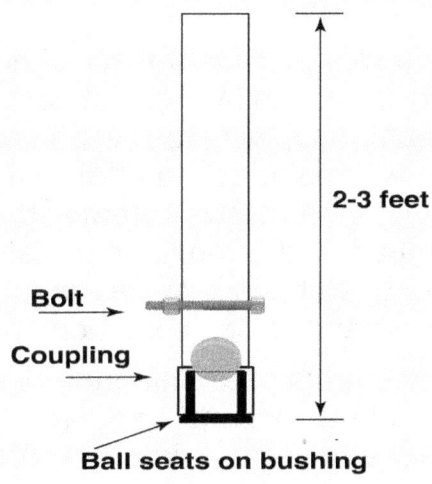

How To Dig And Construct A Well Using A Well Point

Finding water doesn't have to be a complicated process. The invention of the "well point" certainly simplified the process of extracting water for shallow water wells. These days many shallow water tables are susceptible to pollution and the water obtained should really only be considered for irrigation and household chores.
Have your water tested before you use it.

Point Wells

Driving a well point is the act of hitting a screened well point into the earth with a sledgehammer. Once you reach the water table, the well point acts as the well screen and it allows clean water to enter the well and to be pumped to the top. It is a really simple technique for water extraction and it works quite well when the soil conditions permit.

- This method is predominantly used in soil that's rich in thick sand or gravel. Don't use it in soil that consists of hard, red clay or rock.

- It is suitable for areas where the water table is 10-25 feet below the surface.

These well points can be driven 30+ feet into the ground if needed, but that's no easy feat. Check with locals and your local water office to compare the success rate for this method in your area.

It will all come down to soil conditions and depth of water table.

Something to keep in mind is that areas with shallow water tables are more susceptible to contamination from land use. Contaminants can easily seep through the soft, sandy soil into your well, even from distances far away. When planning a "point well" it is best to be at least 150 feet away from potential sources of contamination. These include septic tanks, livestock yards, ponds, sewers, etc. Check with your local government office to get the exact code specifics for your area.

Make sure you test your water before consuming it.

How To

Start by collecting all the material that you will need. You can purchase complete well point kits from hardware stores or from an online merchant. When looking at the materials used, you will notice that all the components are made of metal. This makes galvanized steel your best option. Quality material will not bend, break or rust.

When selecting your well point, remember that a well point of $1\frac{1}{4}$" will suit most wells down to 25 feet.

You will need:

- **A well point**, also called a "Sand point". The well point is a heavy spear-like object that is around 3-5 feet long and $1^1/_4$ to 2" in diameter. It has a metal screen on the outside to prevent larger particles from entering your well and also a fine screen on the inside for smaller particles. If you are planning to go down less than 25 feet, then you can use a $1^1/_4$ well point with metal piping and a shallow-well pump. If you want to go deeper, you will need a 2" well point with metal piping and a deep-well pump installation.

- **Galvanized steel pipe extensions** around 5 feet long. ($1^1/_4$" or 2" in diameter.)

- **Threaded metal couplings.** Try to get long couplings with extra thread.

- **Metal drive cap.** If the drive cap is threaded, the it must be the same diameter as the pipe extensions. Some setups come with a galvanized nipple which is first threaded into the coupling. The drive cap is placed on top of the nipple. Make sure you follow the manufacturer's instructions.

- **Pipe Wrenches x 2.**

- **Carpenter's level or Plumb bob.**

- **Plumber's tape/ Teflon tape.** Wrap it clockwise, with the thread!

- **Sledgehammer.**

- **Auger or post hole digger.**

- **Garden hose.**

- **A long wooden pole** (or similar) for surging the well hole.

- **Pump.** A Pitcher pump is suitable for a $1^1/_4$ pipe and depth of 25 feet.

  A Jet pump is suitable for a 2" pipe and depth of 25-45 feet.

- **An extra pair of hands.** This is a two-man job.

1. Start by making a hole in the ground with an auger or post hole digger. Go down a few feet just to get you started.

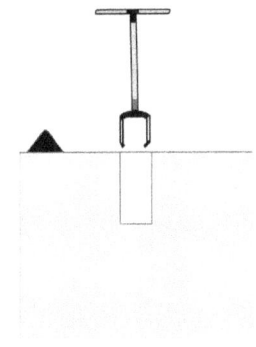

Take the well point and rub a bar of soap over the openings. The soap will clog the holes and prevent debris from entering. Later, the soap will dissolve when you strike water. The soap also makes it easier to drive the point into the ground.

2. Place your well point in the hole.

You will need to add a coupling and pipe extension from the start. Clean the thread first and remember to use Teflon tape (clockwise) and to lock the coupling in place. Use one wrench to hold the pipe in place and the other to tighten the coupling. This is a two-man job.

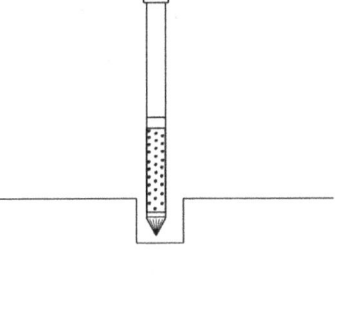

3. Place the drive cap on the pipe. Use the level or plumb bob to make sure that the pipe is vertically lined up in the hole. Drive it into the ground with your sledge-

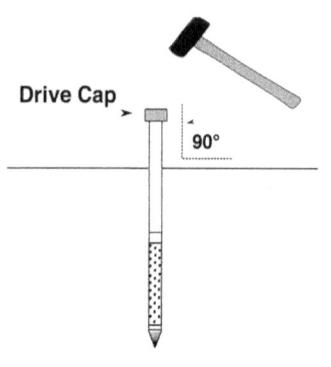

hammer.

The drive cap protects the pipe threads on the well point and provides a better striking surface. Make sure you strike it evenly. It's best to have a helper to help with keeping the pipe perpendicular.

4. Keep on driving the well point, with pipe extension, into the ground. At first, it will be smooth and easy. When there's about $1/2$ foot (15cm) of pipe left sticking out the ground, you can stop to add another section of extension pipe. Repeat this sequence as you go deeper.

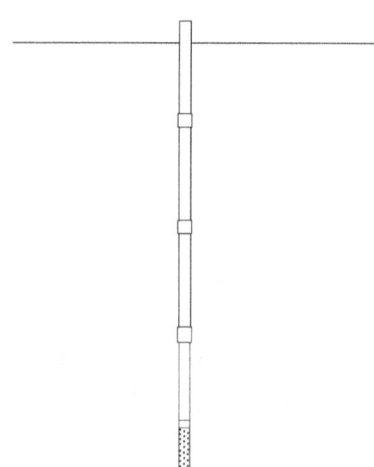

Pour water at regular intervals down the pipe. Wet soil is easier to penetrate.

Remember to use the drive cap when adding the extension pipes.

Check couplings and remember to use Teflon tape.

You can use the plumb bob to try to keep things level

and perpendicular to the ground. You are dealing with a long length of pipe. Do your best to send it straight down into the earth. Repeat till you reach the water table.

If you hit rock, don't try to break it with the well point. Depending on the depth, you can try to move the pipe side to side and to wiggle it to create some annular space around it. If unsuccessful, pull up the pipe and move to a new location. No use destroying your well point.

5. Reaching the water table means that you are in water bearing sand. There are a couple of ways to test if you've reached the water bearing sand.

• When hitting water bearing sand, you will suddenly become aware that it is easier to drive your well point through this section.

• Also, listen for a variation in sound when you strike the cap. If you suddenly start to hear a hollow sound like made by a dinner gong, then you are probably in fine, water-bearing sand.

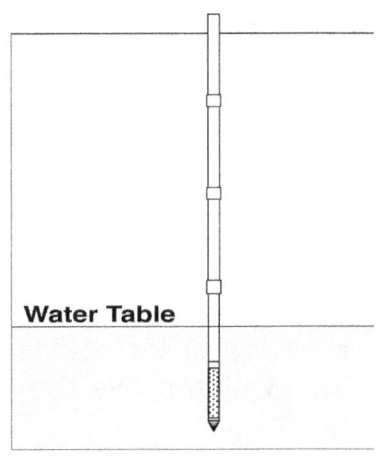

• You can pour water into the top of the pipe. If it sinks down within a short period of time (2 mins), you are in the water table. If

Water Table

it stays at the top, it means that you are still in the soil layer.

If you sense that you have reached the water table, check your notes and compare with your local water table depth that you researched beforehand.

Take a line with a small weight attached and drop it down the pipe. Measure how deep you are into the water table.

6. When you have reached the water table, continue for at least another 8-10 feet if possible. The deeper the better for you want the well screen to be totally submerged in water.

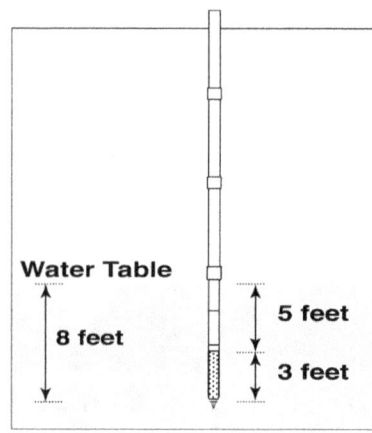

Remember that groundwater is replenished through rain. There are always seasonal variations in rainfall, which means that the level of the water table underground, will also rise and fall. The deeper you go into the water table, the better off you'll be in the dry season.

7. Once you've reached the correct depth you can start to develop the well. This will improve the yield and also the longevity.

You have to clean around the well screen,

to remove the fine particles and to leave only the larger particles behind. The well screen will filter the larger particles.

You can clean the well by using either a surging technique or jet washing it with a garden hose.

a.) To surge, place a long pole down the pipe till below the water level and push up and down to surge the water through the perforated point.

b.) You can push the garden hose all the way down the pipe to jet the particles out.

8. The next step is to attach a pump and a concrete apron at the top of the well. The apron should drain away from the well towards a storm drain.

To avoid well contamination during a flood scenario, you should try to keep your pump at least 3 feet off the ground. This applies to both hand pumps and electric pumps.

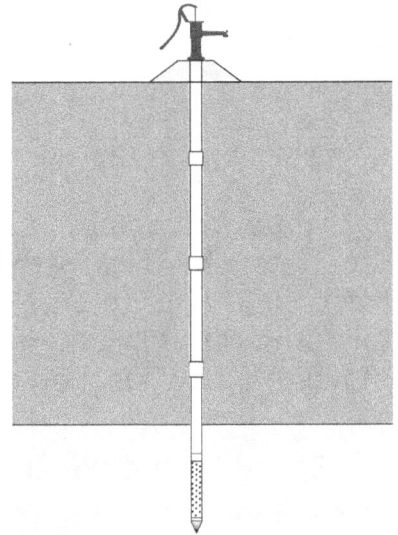

If your pump pipe diameter and the well pipe diameter don't match up, you can fit a reducer coupling to connect the two.

Operate the pump to further remove debris and particles

from around the well screen. This will take a while, but you have to do it till you see clear, clean water coming out the top of the well.

Remember that off-the-shelf hand pumps are mostly used for depths up to 20-25 feet. These pumps have to be primed to get the water from 20 feet down all the way up into the pump.

If you cannot or don't want to prime your pump, then you will need a check valve. This is an inlet valve that is positioned on the horizontal line leading to the pipe. It is a one-way valve that allows water to go up towards the pump, but not down and out.

Having a check valve means that u don't constantly have to prime the hand pump. The result is that you always have water at the ready in the pump.

If you are close to an electrical source then you have an option of installing an electric Jet pump.

Conclusion

Using a well point is a very simple and straightforward method for water extraction. Try not to break the well point by forcing it through the rocky patches. Just move to a new location and start a new hole.

People tend to get excited once they hit water. Be smart and do not drink water from the ground, except if you are 100% sure about the quality. It's always best to test your water before consumption.

All wells need a pump to transport the water to a place of storage. Tanks are perfect vessels for water storage.

Make sure you take a look at a later chapter where we take a closer look at well pump basics.

If you have any health issues, you should first check with your doctor before starting this project.

How To Dig And Construct A Well

The most basic method for extracting water involves digging, with basic tools, through the dry, unsaturated zone. The depth of the water table will decide how deep you have to dig. You have to dig into the water table and line it with a porous material for clean water to enter the well. Line and seal the upper part of the well to prevent cave-ins and contamination.

This is a very dangerous method that should be done with the aid of a professional.

Dug Wells

To dig a well by hand should be a last resort, for desperate times. This method is dangerous, slow, unpredictable and not feasible as a long-term solution. It is also open to contamination which is problematic, to say the least. A shallow water well should be at least 100 feet (30m) from any source of possible contamination. It is this writer's opinion that 150 feet (45m) is a safer distance, since we are experiencing more adverse weather conditions than ever before. There is an increase in floods in certain areas and floods are a well's biggest enemy. See the section on well maintenance at the end of this chapter. When

You will need:

- A shovel and pickax for digging.
- Simple waterproofing plaster.
- Lengths of rope or cable used to lower and haul equipment.
- A winch with head frame to haul heavy objects from well.
- Pulleys for simple lowering and hauling tasks.
- Bailing buckets for hauling dug material from the well.
- Hammers, nails, wood.
- Hard hats.
- Level, plumb bob and plumb line.
- Ladder (rope or rigid).
- Eye protection.
- Medical kit.

selecting a location for your well, consider contamination, the soils, geology, and slope of the land. The well should be located uphill of septic systems, barnyards, livestock pastures, and fuel tanks, and at least 30 feet (10m) from streams and ponds. In addition, wells should not be located in extremely wet areas.

The following design will introduce the basics of well digging and it will give you an idea of all the dynamics at work.
Dug wells work on a simple principle:

- Find an aquifer close to the surface and dig a round hole that extends below the water table level. Never ever dig a square hole. It **will** cave-in!

- Remember to reinforce the well wall as

Well Digging Basics

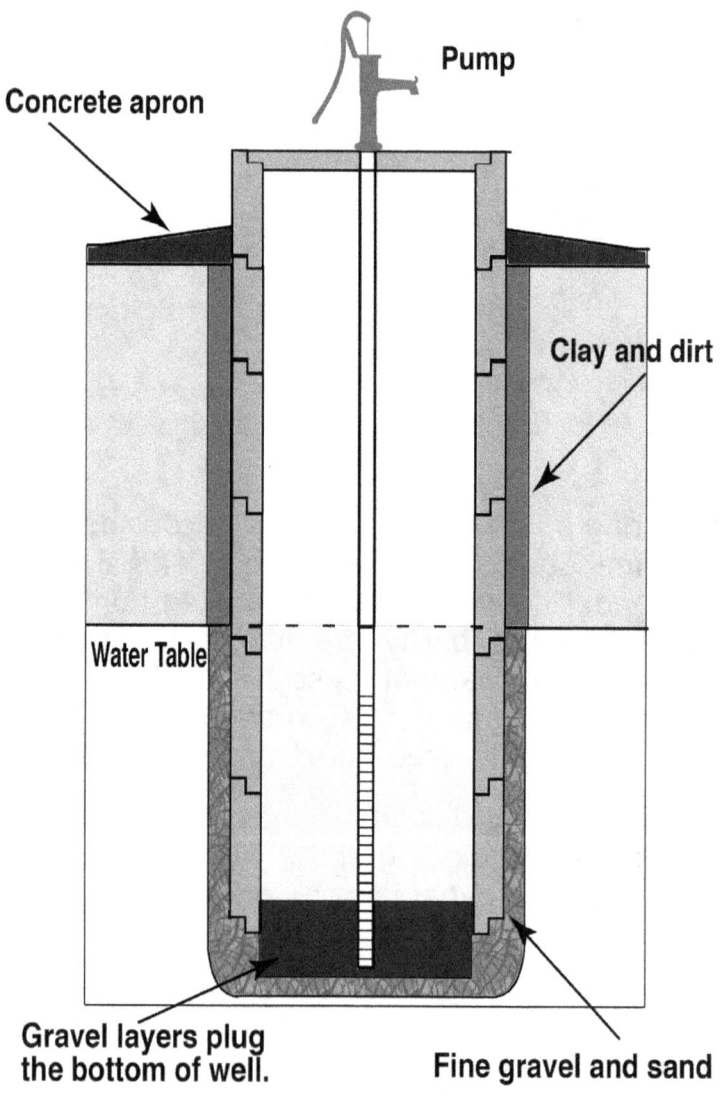

you dig deeper and to remove dirt and debris from the hole. You can reinforce the well wall with bricks or with poured cement.

• Make sure you are below the water table, for this is where water will start to seep through the well wall and to accumulate in the bottom of the hole. Plug the bottom of the well with gravel to keep sediment and large particles out.

That's your well.

This method only works in areas with suitable soil like sand, clay or gravel. In rocky areas with boulders you can forget about it.
On paper, it's definitely possible to use a shovel and pickax to dig a hole and to find water. Unfortunately, the whole process is not as simple as it sounds and it is not recommended doing this on your own. It is, at the very least, a five-man job that requires experience, lots of common sense, and a variety of tools. Basic well digging is a low cost method of well construction, but it is also considered very dangerous due to the possibility of cave-ins. Traditionally these wells for personal use are 4-5 feet in diameter and are dug by hand. Depending on the ground in your area, you can go anywhere from 8-20 feet deep. The method we are going to discuss is considered the easiest, safest and requires fairly simple tools and moving equipment. It involves reinforcing the inside of the well with a concrete well lining, also called a Caisson ring. If digging in

unstable ground, you run the risk of the well wall collapsing.

The best and simplest method is to use pre-cast concrete well rings as your well lining (Caisson rings). These are precast and are about 2" (5cm) thick and 3-5 feet (90-150cm) in diameter. They are similar to the manhole cement rings we see on road construction sites. They should have joints that allow them to "fit" into place. You will need to construct a windlass (winch on tripod or head frame) above your well to assist with the moving of dirt, rocks, concrete rings and bailing of water.

Preparations

There are various ways to dig a well. The use of precast concrete rings has proven to be a very efficient method, but it does involve a fair amount of preparation.

- Prepare your concrete rings. You will have to do some research to see what's available in your area. Discuss in detail what you need and the implementation of the rings. They must be wide enough for a person to stand in. Around 4-5ft (1.2-1.5m) will do. Remember to determine the depth of the water table beforehand. This will give you an indication of how many rings you require. You will also need professional lifting equipment.

Do not attempt to move/lift a concrete ring without proper lifting equipment as prescribed by the manufacturer!

- These rings are heavy and it will be an arduous and a dangerous task to move them around. Each ring must be safely position over the well hole and to do this, you will need a **forklift** and a truck. There is no way around this.

A standard ring has at least two "lifting holes" (through the side) which are used for hoisting and lowering. Make sure you get rings with **lifting holes** on the inside or with holes that go straight through the sides. Use the correct lifting straps and lifting keys/ hooks. Don't rig any ropes around or on the underside of the ring. Once your well is finished, remember to seal off all holes where potential contaminants can enter.

- You should have a **sturdy platform** constructed around the opening of the well hole.

When you are ready to sink the first concrete ring, place two thick pieces of timber over the hole. You can rest your first concrete ring on top. Once ready, lift the ring, remove the timber, and slowly lower the ring into the hole.

This part of the process will require patience and teamwork. Make sure that safety is a first priority.

- You will need **lifting equipment**. Moving material in and out of the well is no simple task. Take care that your lifting equipment is not too heavy, for that can also cause the top of the well to collapse. Use a heavy-duty **electric winch with head frame** for heavy objects and a simple pulley system (or windlass) for buckets filled with dirt. It is not advisable to lower the cement rings by hand. The process of hauling and lowering material is a very dangerous one. This is where most accidents occur.

The head frame can also act as windlass and should have a solid platform underneath (wood) to prevent objects from being knocked into the well hole.

• You will need **waterproofing plaster** to seal the top ten feet of the well. This is to prevent contaminants from entering the clean well water.

It is not necessary to plaster the bottom section of the well. This part is submerged in the water-bearing sand of the water table and you want the water to enter through the openings between the concrete rings.

• **Organize your well.** Draw up a plan with the layout of the construction areas. This should include the dumping area, no-driving zone, no-contamination zone, washing area, rest area, tool storage, etc.

• You will have to prepare a **dumping area** well away from the well hole. This is where all the material taken from the well will be dumped.

Calculate how much space you'll need by determining the volume of dirt that must be excavated from the well. Make sure that the daily routine of moving the dirt will not cause the well sides to collapse.

• **Prepare storage space** for construction tools. Tools should be locked away when not in use.

• **Create a path system for workers** to follow. This creates a safe environment with designated areas for work and rest.

• The construction team should be **well trained** and everybody should know his or her task(s) and what equipment they are responsible for. Use a system of hand signals when communicating with diggers inside the well.

How To

1. Start by digging a hole wide enough for you to stand in.
Remember that your concrete ring has to fit inside this hole. Around 4-5ft (1.2-1.5m) will do. Keep the diameter of the hole in mind and leave the wall curves nice and smooth.
At this stage, nothing should be suspended or hanging above the digger.

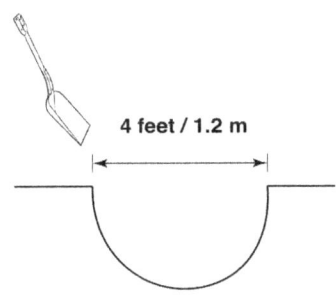

2. Go down to about 3 feet (1m) and stop to inspect your hole.
The first cutting ring

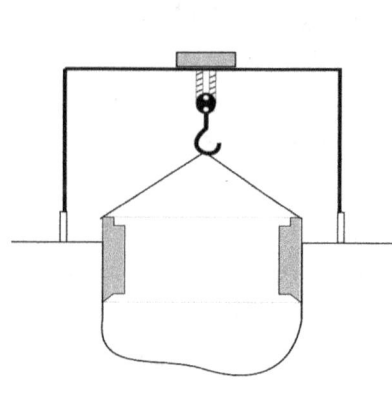

should be able to fit snugly inside. Typically, the first well ring has a "cutting edge" to scrape away the dirt.

Dig down to a depth that will allow the first well ring to sit level in the well.

CAUTION! When lowering these rings, all workers should be safely outside of the well!

3. Once the ring has been lowered, a worker can be allowed to go down and to stand inside the hole. While standing inside the ring, start to excavate underneath it; as you remove the dirt, the ring's weight will allow it to sink deeper into the hole. Remove the soil gently and evenly from underneath the ring. This will allow the ring to slide in a level position down the well.

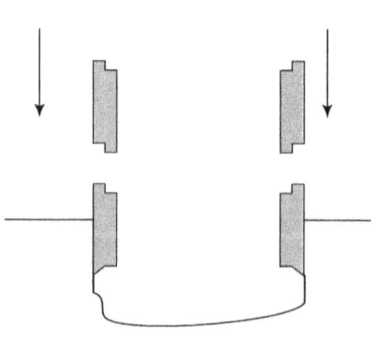

Just allow it to slide down a few inches. You have to leave the upper part of the ring exposed to join the second ring. Gently lower the second ring and make sure that the joints line up.

Remember that once the hole is completed, you will have to seal the **upper joints** of the well with waterproofing plaster!

4. The next step is very important.

Connect the second ring to the first ring with metal rods or chains.

This can be achieved by placing a metal connection inside the "lifting eye" of the ring. This method will aid in sending the whole column of rings down evenly and in a rigid, straight line.

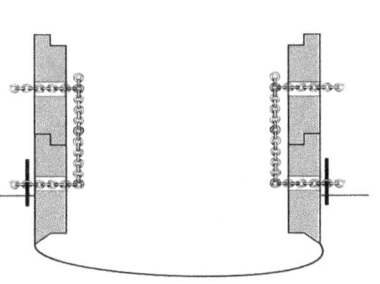

5. Level. Use a level or plumb-bob (a weight on a string) to check your progress and if you are digging in a straight line.

Do this routinely as you go deeper.

The stack of rings must slide evenly, at a ninety degree angle, down the hole.

6. Keep on stacking these rings on top of one another till you reach the water table.

All the rings should be in a column, tightly fastened with rods or chains.

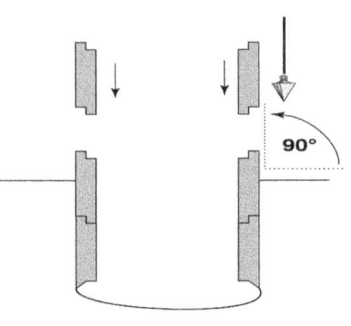

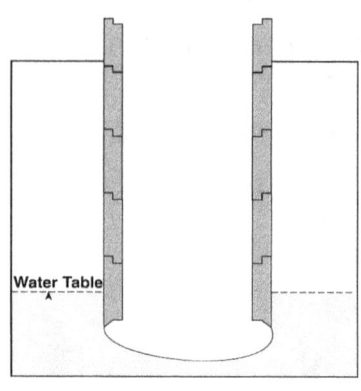

This is no easy feat and you will have to pay close attention to the task at hand. At this stage, the help of an expert will come in very handy. For a novice, this can be considered as on-the-job training and it will require some perseverance.

Patience is key and it will undoubtedly take a qualified person to guide you through this process. Upon reaching the water table, you have to stop.

7. Pump or bail. Once you reach the water table, you can expect water to start seeping into the bottom of the well. This is where digging gets hard and where you will get wet.

Try to go as deep as you can. At least 5 feet more. You will have to pump or bail the water from the well.

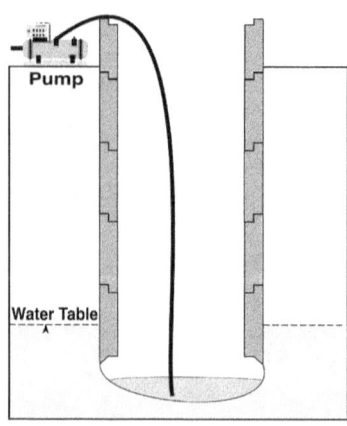

When using a pump and generator, take care that the generator is downwind and that it is not sending fumes down into your hole.

8. Gravel. Once you find that the flow rate of water into the well is faster than the bailout rate, then you have to stop. You are now truly under the water table. (You should aim to be at least 5 feet under the water table.) Fill the bottom of the well with gravel.

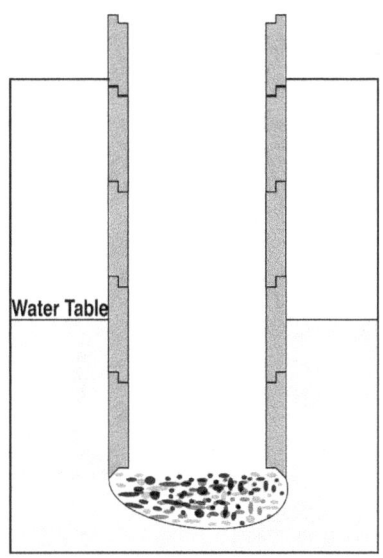

One foot of gravel will do nicely. Use coarse gravel as a top layer and fine gravel underneath. Fill it up properly to prevent clay and other sludgy material from entering the well. Clean water can penetrate into the well from the porous sides and from the bottom filled with gravel.

9. Protection. Seal the top 10ft (3m) of well rings on the inside with a waterproof concrete sealant to create an effective seal against contaminants that might seep in through the adjacent soil on the outside.

10. Annular space. Fill any openings on the outside of the concrete ring casings (top 10 feet) with clay or concrete. This is to prevent surface water contamination. This is of great importance!

11. Seal the well. At the top of your well,

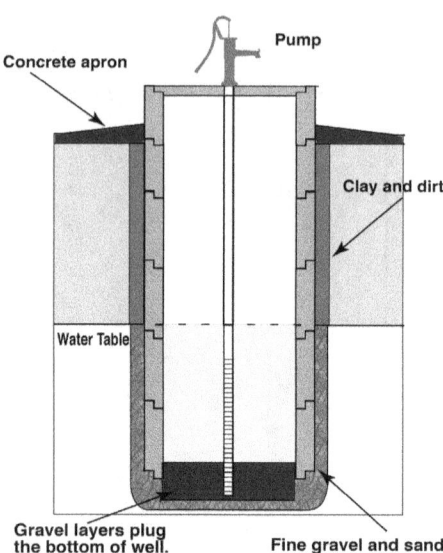

you want the well lining to extend about 3 feet (1m) above ground. This is where you have to consider contamination. Make sure that no contaminants can seep into your well, whether through the well opening at the top or through the adjacent soil.

To seal your well top you can create an apron from reinforced concrete. Make sure that it runs downhill and that it drains water away from the well into a storm drain or another collection area. This apron should be reinforced, strong and wide (6 feet of space all around). This is where people walk and where water containers are filled. Cracks in the apron will cause contaminants to seep into your well.

12. Pumps. Install a hand pump at the top of your well. Remember that off-the-shelf hand pumps are mostly used for depths up to 20-25 feet. These pumps have to be primed to get the water from 20 feet down all the way up into the pump. If you don't want to prime your pump, then you

How to lower concrete rings in a level position?

- Digging method: When scraping the dirt away from underneath the ring, start by making four fist-sized holes in the 3, 6, 9, 12 o'clock positions. Next, make four holes in between the previous four created. Make eight holes in between the existing holes created. Your ring should start to slide down while doing this.

- Join the concrete rings together as you lay them on top of each other. This creates a unit of rings that slide down the wall in a straight line. You can join the rings with bolts, chains or lap joints.

will need a foot valve. This is an inlet valve that is positioned at the bottom, suction end of the well pipe. It is a one-way valve that allows water to go up towards the pump, but not down and out. Having a foot valve means that u don't constantly have to prime the hand pump. The result is that you always have water at the ready in the pump.

If you are close to an electrical source then you have an option of installing an electric Jet pump.

Other Options

You can consider alternative well casing support. The main issue is safety. In loose soil, the concrete ring method is best. This basic method allows water to enter the well from the bottom. However, once inside the water table, you have the following alternatives:

a.) There are porous concrete rings available that can be used within the water table to let water in. Tiny holes in the concrete wall will keep sediment out and let water in.

b.) Concrete rings with holes (slanted upwards) can also be used within the water table. The holes must be angled upwards from the outside in. This aids in keeping sediment out.

When concrete well casings are not an option, you can consider the following methods:

- Clay bricks can be used in stable ground

Benefits of using precast concrete rings

- They are strong, durable and ideal for use as a well lining.

- Using concrete rings cuts down on manpower needed.

- They can be sealed with waterproofing plaster to prevent contaminated surface water from seeping in.

- They cut down on excavation time.

- They will not corrode or rust and will not contaminate the water in the well.

- They come in different sizes are considered safe to use by the industry.

- They are perfectly round, lock into place and provide good structural strength.

and at shallow depths. You have to dig as deep as possible before you start laying the bricks. This method requires stacking bricks from the bottom of the well (within the water table) and it means getting wet and bailing water by hand or with a pump. This method is for experts only.

• Various molds (Brit. moulds) can be used to pour concrete that can act as the well lining. You can dig down to around 10 feet, create a mold from wood or sheet (corrugated) metal, and then pour your concrete. The concrete will set in between the mold and the soil of the well wall. This will also require the help of an expert.

• In very stable soil, and with a fairly shallow well, you also have the option of digging the shaft first. Afterwards, you can slide the concrete rings down. This is also a dangerous method and not recommended. In stable soil and hard rock, the risk of a cave-in is lower.

Conclusion

Some of the biggest issues with wells of this nature is safety awareness and prevention of contamination. A deep, open hole has the potential to cause accidents, not just to workers, but to anybody who ventures onto the construction site. Wherever humans and machines are involved, we find an immediate rise in pollution levels and also in contamination of the environment. Extra care must be taken to guarantee a safe, contaminant-free environment. Part of being aware of contamination is instructing the excavation foreman to implement excavation guidelines. These guidelines will include work schedules, safety procedures, emergency procedures, waste disposal, workplace etiquette, etc.

Summary

Having a well can be a very rewarding experience, but just how rewarding will depend on a couple of factors.

- Make sure that your well is fully developed. Once your well installation is complete, all cuttings and sediment must be removed to ensure that water can freely enter the well.

- Check that your bore-hole has no stability issues. The well should be sealed and the well casing, screen and pump system should be made of quality material. Cracked pipes or screens will require drilling a new well.

- Watch for over-pumping. This occurs when water is withdrawn at a faster rate than it can be replenished. It is a common problem with wells and it leads to premature well failure.

- Watch out for dissolved gas (nitrogen, methane), corrosive water and biofouling. Water saturated with oxygen can cause bacterial growth, which causes a biofilm to develop inside the well. This can mean reduced well yield and water quality.

Dug Wells and Safety Concerns

- Place a fence around the well to keep ALL animals, no matter how big or small, out of the well. A scorpion or snake can kill you.
- Place a fence or barrier to keep people, especially children, out.
- During the construction period, place a lid on the well opening when the construction site is abandoned.
- Always leave a safety line in the well, in case someone were to fall in. This line should be a sturdy rope, twice as long as your planned well depth.
- Make sure that the digger wears a hardhat or helmet when in the hole.
- Check that all ropes are new and not worn.
- Check that bucket handles are secure and that the bottoms of the buckets have no cracks.
- Get a pair of steel-capped boots to protect your toes. Using shovels in a confined space increases the chance of accidents.
- Knots should be double-checked.
- Protect the top of the well by placing some wooden planks all along the edge of the well hole. This will prevent workers from wearing away the ground around the well.
- Always keep a safety kit on site.
- Toilets and washing areas should be 75 feet away from your well.
- Plan ahead where vehicles and forklifts will be allowed to drive. Do not disturb soil around your well's edge.
- When using generators, make sure that fumes are downwind of the well hole.
- The attitude of all workers should be professional and alert. Do not joke around a well site and do not allow alcohol or other mind-altering substances to be consumed while working.

CHAPTER 04

The Basics Of Wells and Water Pumps

Pumps are used to "pull" or "push" water from a water source to a holding tank or to directly feed the household plumbing. Typically, the water source can be a well, spring or a pond. Pump installations should be done by a licensed professional to make sure that you get the most out of your pump. A correctly installed pump will last long, use very little energy and deliver water with optimum flow rate and pressure.

Your well must be fully developed and pumped clean of large particles, debris and fine sand before you install the pump; no use clogging your pump or pipes with sediment or drill cuttings.

To select the appropriate pump for your water volume needs, you will have to consider the following:

   a.) The water level of the water in the well.

   b.) The diameter of your well pipe.

   c.) The number of plumbing fixtures (water

Connecting An Electric Pump

A pump is used to draw water from the well and to move it to a new location. Selecting the right pump for your needs, will depend on the following:

1. The estimated **volume** of water you need for your property.

2. The **power source** you will connect to. Pumps can connect to the power grid, batteries, solar panels or generators.

3. The **environment**. A harsh environment with dry and dusty conditions will require a quality pump with screen and shield protection.

consuming appliances) that require water.

d.) The volume of water required in gallons per minute (gpm) during peak water demand.

e.) Your preferred power source. (Connected to the grid or solar.)

These are questions that every well owner should be knowledgeable about.

Different pumps are used for different applications and it's vital to select the correct pump for your needs.

Pump Basics

Depending on the aforementioned conditions, you can consider looking at the following types of pumps:

• **Jet pumps** are, generally speaking, suitable for wells that are 3 inches or less in diameter.

- *Shallow well jet pumps* are often used for shallow water wells which are no deeper than 25 feet. The pump is located at surface level.

- *Deep well jet pumps* work well with wells as deeper as 80-100 feet. The jet is located inside the well, below the water level.

• **Submersible pumps** are long cylindrical pumps (with motor) around 2-3 feet long. They are used in wells 3 inches or more in diameter.
Submersible pumps are very efficient pumps with high yield and high delivery pressure.

Check Valves And Foot Valves

One-way valves are a very important component of the pump system. The use of one-way valves prevents the water from flowing back down into the well and it ensures that the pump is primed.

• There are two options for jet pumps:

- Usually, a **foot valve** is placed at the end of the suction line, which is at the bottom-end of the well. They are mostly used in drilled wells.

Having the foot valve at the bottom of the well can be problematic, because it's hard to get to for maintenance purposes.

- A **check valve** is a good option (especially for driven wells) and can be installed in the feed line next to the pump. This assures that the pump line and pump is filled with water when the pump is switched off. If you put your check valve next to the pump, above ground, then you need an additional fitting above ground (at the top of the suction line) to prime the pump.
You can use $1^1/_4$ inch male PVC adapters with the valve.

• For submersible pumps we use check valves where needed. Usually submersible pumps come with a check valve pre-installed in the pump that you place at the bottom of the well. If your well is very deep, install a check valve for every 150 - 200 feet (45-60m) of pipe. You should also have a check valve at surface level to ensure a steady flow of water to your distribution system.

Pressure Tanks

Pumps work very well in combination with pressure tanks.
The function of the pressure tank in a water well system is to create water pressure by using compressed air to push down on the water in the tank.
The pressure tank functions as a reservoir and holds enough pressure to flush a toilet in the house, without turning the pump on.

- The normal operating pressure ranges for pumps are 20/40, 30/50, 40/60 or even as high as 60/80 psi. This means that pressure is kept constant within a 20 psi range, which sets a boundary for starting and stopping the pump.

A 40/60 ratio is recommended since it's by far the best ratio to keep a constant shower stream. This pressure range indicates when the pump will turn on and off, and this function is controlled by a pressure switch device. This is the device that will turn your pump on and off automatically.

Example: If you have a 40/60 psi setting, the pump will turn on when the pressure in the pressure tank drops to around 40 psi and off when the pressure reaches 60 psi.

The relationship between the pressure switch, pressure tank and the pump is what allows water to flow through the pipes in your home. When selecting a pressure tank, you will need to know the performance of the pump in gallons per minute.

- We measure the volume of water required to serve a household, in gallons per minute (gpm). It is calculated by looking at the water consuming appliances in the house and also at the pump's flow rate in gpm.

The gpm of the pump must equal the total number of water consuming appliances.

Example:

5 faucets, 2 toilets, a shower and a washing machine would require 9 gpm.

• To determine the appropriate size of the tank, match the draw down of the tank to the capacity of the pump.

Another easy way to size a tank, is to take the gpm system requirement that you determined for your house, and to multiply it by 3 and then to go to the next largest tank size.

In our previous example:

9 (gpm) x 3 = 27.

Buy a 30 gallon or bigger pressure tank.

Usually, when it comes to pressure tanks, bigger is better. A larger pressure tank will not hurt your pump's performance, but it will give you a larger draw down capacity, which guarantees even more usable pressure in the plumbing system, before the pump needs to come on.

• In general, a $1/2$ HP pump is enough for a small house with one bathroom and a couple of people.
For a larger house, you'll need a $3/4$ -1 HP pump.

• Take into consideration that a larger pump will affect your electricity bill and that it will also require a larger pressure tank.

• If you want a generator as a back-up

power source, make sure that the generator can provide enough power to start the pump.

Pitless Adapters

In colder climates where water pipes should be protected from freezing, a pitless adapter is used to keep the water, pumped from your well, **under the frost line and in a sanitary environment**.
Installing a pitless adapter is a much better option than using the old well pits we still see in certain parts of the world today.
Although a pitless adapter can be used with standard jet pumps, they are commonly used with submersible pumps, where the pressure tank is located in a pump house or basement.
This adapter consists of a special fitting that is installed 6-10 ft (2-3 m) below ground level for protection from frost.
A hole is made in the well casing and the water coming up from the

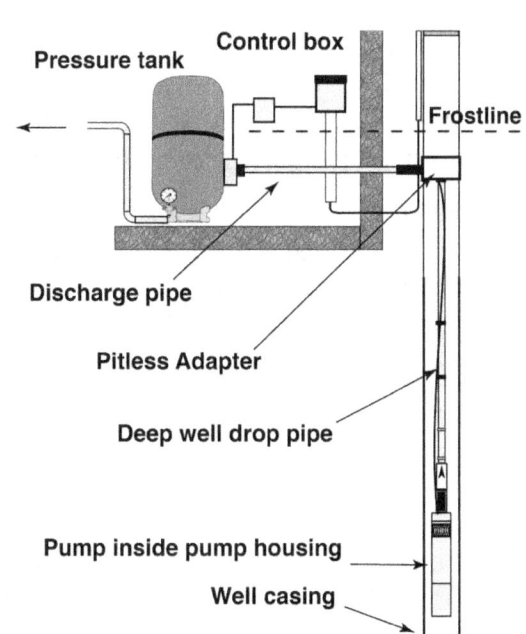

The Basics Of Wells and Water Pumps

well is diverted horizontally at the adapter, and discharged into a water pipe that runs underground to the house or pump house.

The main benefit of these adapters are:

- These adapters are cheap and reduce the risk of contamination in your well.

- A pitless adapter makes it easy to access the well for routine maintenance or emergency service.

The Basics Of A Shallow Well Jet Pump

Depth: 10-25 feet
Expected life: 10 years

For a shallow water well you will need a simple jet pump. Jet pumps are relatively inexpensive and require little maintenance. Expect your jet pump to last an average of ten years. Some basic information about jet pumps:

- Simple, **shallow well jet pumps** can draw water up to 25 feet. They do not work with deeper wells. For a deeper well you will need a **deep well jet pump**.
- Jet pumps can also be used as booster pumps to improve the existing pressure to a higher level.

Mechanics

These pumps are easy to operate and basically "suck" the water out of the well. When we say suck, it actually means that the pressure from our atmosphere is pressing down on the water and pushing it up the well pipe.

When you turn on the pump, it creates suction in the well pipe and with the push from the atmosphere, the water is jetted up the pipe. Inside the pump, the impeller pushes water through a narrow jet which is a cone-shaped device which creates a vacuum with suction. This is the suction that draws water from the well into the pumping system. The sudden decrease in diameter causes the water to shoot through the jet and eventually out the pump at end use.

Typical shallow well jet pump setup

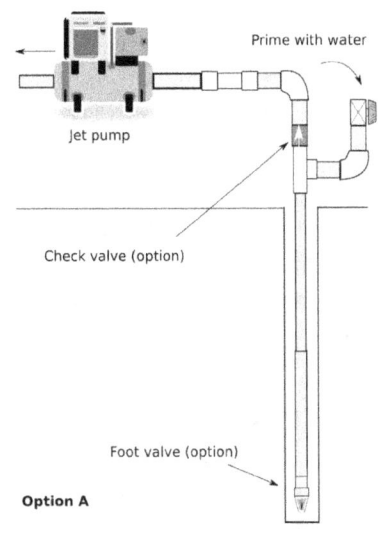

Option A

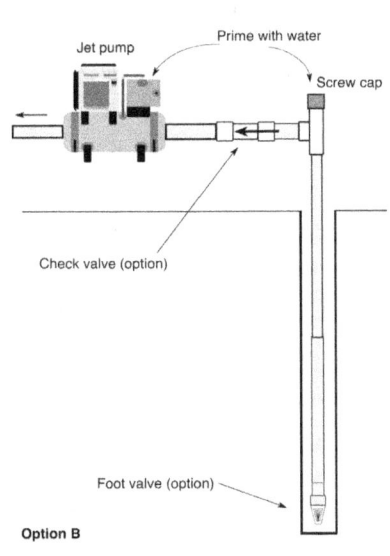

Option B

The Basics Of Wells and Water Pumps

You can install your pump at ground level, above or next to the well hole.

Installation and priming

Before you install your jet pump, make sure that your well is clean and ready to be connected to the pump.

Your well should have a sanitary seal on top of the suction (well) pipe. This should fit your well diameter.

You can also, if needed, make the well head area frost proof with a concrete containment area.

To prevent air pockets, make sure that the pipe slopes slightly downward from the pump to well.

Basic installation of a jet pump.

1. Make sure there's no debris and large particles in the well.

2. Assemble the pump as per manufacturer's instructions. Make sure that you follow the instructions to the letter.

3. Install a $1\frac{1}{4}$ inch foot valve at the bottom of the suction pipe if this is an option. This will suit wells that have easy access to the well pipe like a drilled well.

Another option, as seen with driven wells where the well casing is used as the suction pipe, is to install a $1\frac{1}{4}$ inch check valve in the feed line. You can do it near the pump, in the horizontal or vertical position.

Shallow water pumps generally need to be

primed to work. This is the process of flushing and forcing water into the pump in order to create enough pressure for it to work.

1. Make sure that the pump is turned off.

2. Locate the priming plug and unscrew it.

3. Use a funnel and slowly pour water in. The pump head should be completely filled with water. The water primes and lubricates the pump. When priming, remember that you want the pump and suction pipe to be completely filled with water.

4. Replace the plug once the pump head is completely full.

5. Turn on the pump. Check for leaks.

6. Optionally, you can also give yourself the option of being able to prime the well pipe if needed.

To connect the well pipe to the pump, use a Tee fitting with a threaded cap on top. This is where you can prime the pipe by filling it with water.

The Basics Of A Deep Well Jet Pump

Depth: 25-110 feet
Expected life: 10 years

If your well's water level is deeper than 25 feet, you can look at a deep well jet pump to "push" your water to the surface.
Deep well jet pumps are slightly different from

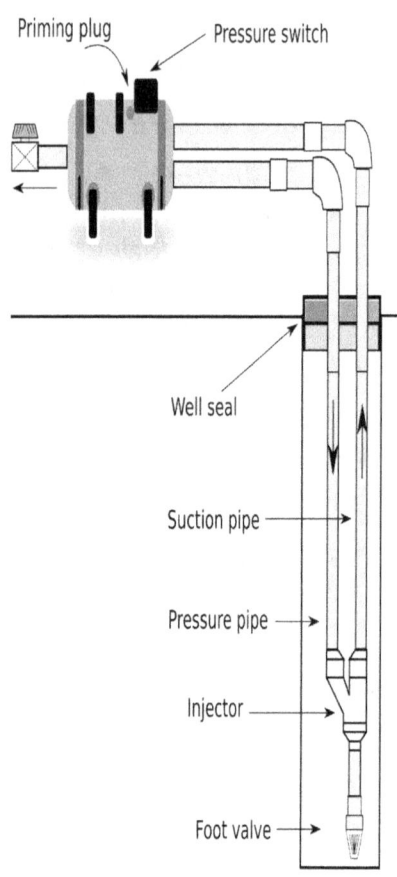

shallow well jet pumps in that they use two water lines in the well, instead of one.
Expect your jet pump to last an average of ten years.

Mechanics

This pump is not as complicated as it looks and uses a very simple method to extract water from a well.
A deep well jet pump works similar to a shallow well jet pump, but the main difference is that the jet is separated from the motor and placed at the bottom of the well. This pump uses a system of two pipes; the one pipe is mounted to the impeller housing and "pushes" water down into the well and into the jet body. The jet is located about 15 feet below the minimum water level. On the output side of the jet body, the second pipe drives the water from the jet back up to the pump and on to a storage tank or to the

household plumbing.

A foot valve is placed at the bottom of the well piping. This foot valve keeps the system primed and prevents draining of water from the pipes.

The jet uses suction and the impeller creates pressure. The combination of these two forces creates a simple application that can produce water lift from 25-110 feet deep.

The Basics Of A Submersible Deep Well Pump

Depth: 25-400 feet
Expected life: 25 years

Submersible pumps are placed inside the well (or water source) and are used to "push" the water to the surface.

Pushing water takes up less energy than pulling water, especially in a deep well.

Mechanics

These are very effective pumps that consist of a pump motor and a series of impellers that are placed inside a cylindrical shape. When turned on, the impellers spin, and this causes the water to be pulled into the pump, which pushes the water to the surface for storage. The pump uses electrical wires that connect to a power source above ground. Note that a pump with three wires plus a GROUND, is a single-phase pump and it requires a control

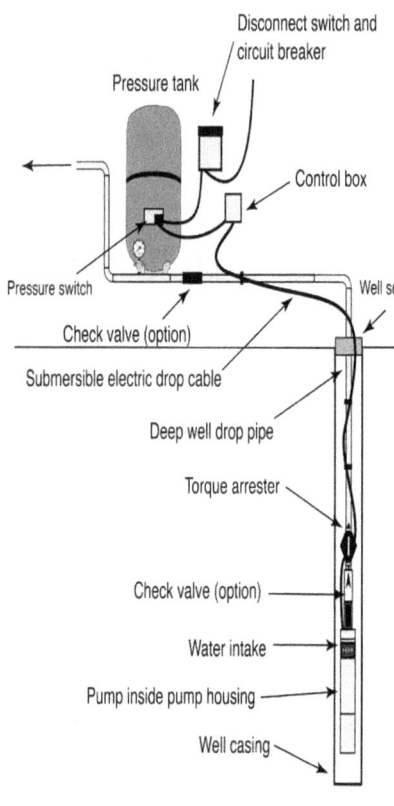

box. The control box is matched to the pump motor. Two wire plus GROUND pump/motor assemblies do not require a control box. Submersible pumps are very reliable and all working parts are sealed within the cylinder. They do not need priming and deliver great volume and pressure. These pumps can deliver water at pretty much any working delivery rate, depending on well depth, pipe diameter and pump horsepower.

Submersible well pumps are typically seen with horsepower ratings of $1/2$ HP, $3/4$ HP, 1 HP, and $1 1/2$ HP.

Pay attention to the following:

- Follow the instructions of the pump manufacturer. Make sure that you are installing the correct pump for your needs.

- When following the manufacturer's instructions, make sure that you get the correct diameter drop pipe to connect to your pipe.

The pump's discharge rate in gpm, must match the diameter of the pipe.

Example: A 10 gpm pump can handle a 1" pipe up to 300 ft.

- All electrical wiring, connections and system grounding must comply with local codes and ordinances.

If unsure, hire an electrician to assist with the electric installation.

- Submersible pumps should be installed 5 feet or more from the bottom of the well.

- Make sure that you use the correct pipe size and material for the well depth, pump type and water quality.

- When cables are spliced and connected, make sure that they are water tight. Besides crimping the wires together, they can also be soldered for an even more secure connection.

- Pumps usually come with a built-in check valve.

For very deep wells, you will have to use a check valve every 150 - 200 feet (45-60m).

Check valves prevent water from flowing back down into the well when the pump shuts off.

They also ensure immediate water flow into the tank when the pump starts up, which prevents unnecessary physical strain on the pump.

- When selecting a submersible pump, pay

special attention to the hermetic seal that protects the electric motor from water.

• The pressure switch senses the pressure coming through from the well and automatically turns the pump on or off.

• Attach a poly safety rope to your pump. You do not want to loose it down the well hole.

• Another safety feature is a torque arrestor.

This is basically a rubber support that clamps to the outside of the pipe and the top of the pump with hose clamps.

The torque arrestor protects the submerged system against the twisting force of the motor as it starts. This prevents unnecessary rotation of the pipe threads.

Absorbing the thrust of the motor also keeps the pump centered in the well casing.

Submersible pumps are great pumps, but remember that the pump must first be pulled from the casing for repairs.
These days the submersible pumps are of a high standard and very reliable.
Pumps can last for 25 years before requiring any form of maintenance.

Connecting A Solar Water Pump

Solar powered water pumps have become very popular as of late and are often used for agricultural operations where conventional power systems are absent. The modern solar energy appliances have been demonstrated to reliably produce electricity and are considered ideal for rural, off-grid scenarios that include irrigation, livestock and domestic use. New technology is making this a very exciting field and the future is looking bright. When buying a new solar powered water pump, make sure that you understand what you are buying, how it works and how it can be modified to suit your needs. Solar powered pumps are different from the regular AC powered pumps in that they use DC power. DC powered pumps are a very good option and they do not require large bursts of power like AC pumps do. Very much like conventional pumps, we find that solar water pumps can be divided into two categories: Surface pumps and Submersible pumps.

- Surface pumps are installed on the outside of the water source (well, spring, pond) and rely on a suction pipe to "suck" the water to the pump and then to "push" the water to the holding tank.

- Submersible pumps are installed under water (well, spring, pond) and "push" the water up to the holding tank

When installing a solar powered pump system, keep in mind that it is an integrated system that consists of various components.
For best performance, buy compatible components from a supplier who is knowledgeable about the complete system setup and the

Solar Pump Basics 1

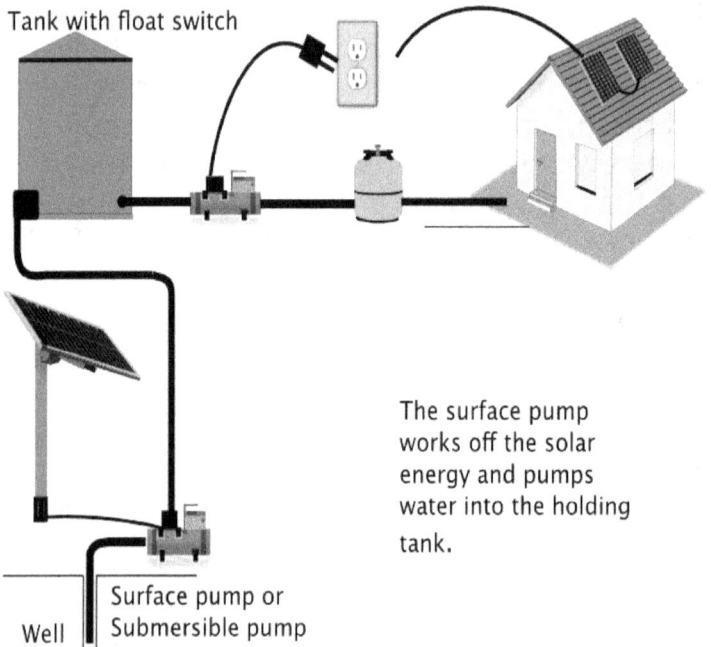

variables that need consideration.

In considering energy efficiency, remember that pumps are better at "pushing" than "sucking", and always keep the distance between the pump and the water at end use as short as possible.

There are two options worth considering:

1. You can power your pump directly with energy obtained from your solar panels (See Solar Pump Basics 1). This means that the pump will only work when the sun is shining. To make it a viable option, you can store your water (as you pump

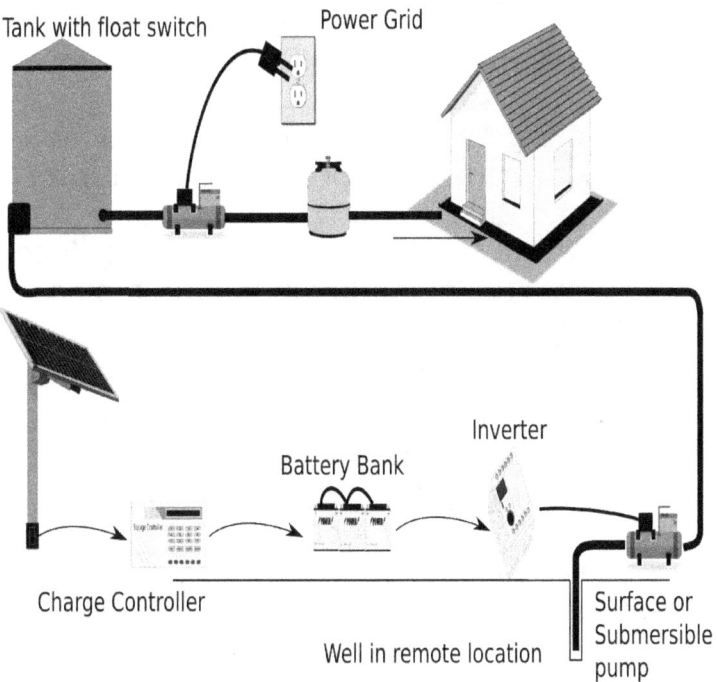

it) in a holding tank and use it when needed. Use a float switch in your tank to shut off the pump when full, and to turn it on when the water drops below a certain level. This is a very simple and effective option.

2. You can store the energy obtained from the solar panels in a battery bank and then rely on the batteries to power your pump (See Solar Pump Basics 2). Having a battery bank allows for additional pumping during the night or when there's no sunlight available. This is a more complicated option.

<u>If your household relies on a tank to provide water to the plumbing system, then you can consider the following options:</u>

- **Booster pump** (See Solar Pump Basics 3). Solar can still provide further solutions. A DC booster pump, powered by solar panels, can assist in providing pressurized water for your home. Booster pumps are to be installed after a storage tank in the water feed line. As mentioned earlier, if your pumping installation is not properly planned, you will not receive satisfactory water service.

- **Gravity feed.** This is a system where you rely on gravity to provide water pressure in your plumbing system. Basically, the higher your tank above the outlets, the more pressure it supplies to the pipes. Gravity offers the advantage of using free energy to produce pressure, however, the tank must be elevated to a height that will deliver sufficient pressure. As a general rule, every foot of elevation provides 0.433 psi of pressure. This means that if the tank is 100 feet (30m) high, it will provide 43 psi of water pressure for your house (100' x 0.433 = 43.3 psi). That kind of elevation is not practical, but some elevation can be achieved by constructing a water tower or by placing the tank uphill of the house. Looking at the math side of things, it's obvious that gravity feed does not offer a realistic solution for the modern home. It can still be used for irrigation and other agricultural purposes.

Solar Pump Basics 3

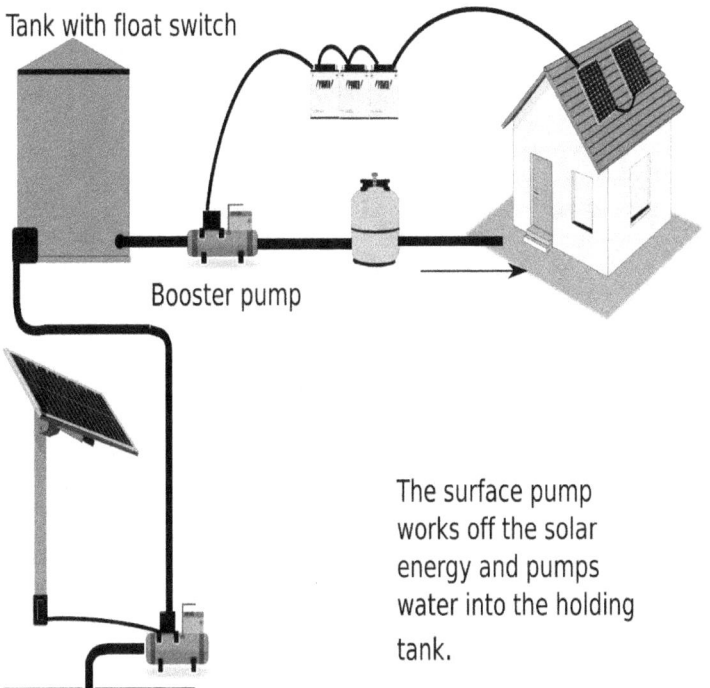

The surface pump works off the solar energy and pumps water into the holding tank.

- **Pressure tank** (See Solar Pump Basics 4). A pressure tank can also be utilized to provide water with enough pressure for your household. Water can be pumped directly from your well, with the solar powered pump, to a pressure tank where it is subsequently stored. The pressure tank is charged by the pump and this maintains pressure in the system, to the point of use in your home.

When buying your solar powered pump, you first have to calculate the lift required to get water out of your well, as

Solar Pump Basics 4

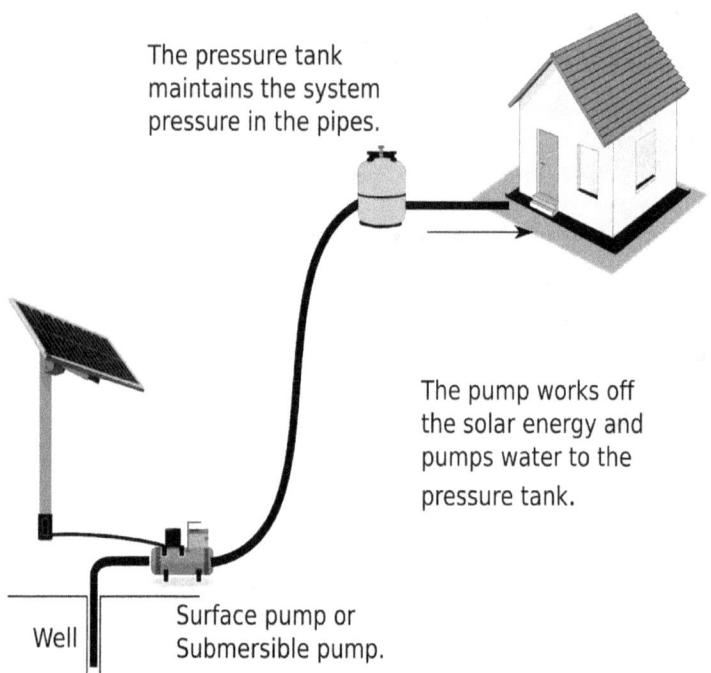

The pressure tank maintains the system pressure in the pipes.

The pump works off the solar energy and pumps water to the pressure tank.

Well

Surface pump or Submersible pump.

well as the distance the water has to be pumped horizontally. This will determine which pump and which setup will provide the best, practical solution.

General Pump Maintenance

Always keep an eye on your well and your pump. Having a pump house, to keep your pump and well head protected from the elements, is a good option.

Pay attention to the following:

- Surface pumps should be three feet above ground level to prevent contamination during flooding and in a location with ventilation and drainage. Pumps should be allowed to breathe and not be covered in leaves or debris.

- Protect your pump and piping from freezing. If severe cold is forecast, drain your pump and remove it from the system.

- Get used to the sound of the pump motor as it pumps. A change in rhythm or unfamiliar hum may point to an issue.

- If possible, try to keep well screens clean and unclogged. This will ensure a steady flow of water and reduce friction and "laboring" in your pump.

- Make sure that your pump is securely fastened to its base. Fasten crews and make sure that there are no cracks in the surrounding cement or sealant. For submersible pumps, tether your pump to a safety rope.

- Keep all waste, chemicals and organic debris away from the system to prevent contamination.

- Be wary of any changes in water color, taste, or smell, as these and other signs may indicate a potentially dangerous issue.

- Only use galvanized steel and Schedule 40 PVC pipe and fittings for surface pumps.

- Electric pumps are not to be "experimented" with. Never tamper with the wiring of your pump. Only a licensed professional should do the work.

Conclusion

Simple is good. Make sure that you are familiar with the operation of the pump and follow all maintenance and safety guidelines to increase the pump's longevity. A simple and efficient pump setup will include a pump that feeds a storage tank with a floating switch.
A second booster pump can be used to provide pressured water from the storage tank to the household plumbing.
Before installing a new pump, check the performance rating chart to make sure it can provide you with the pumping capacity and pressure that you require. Typically, 3-4 gpm is a minimum acceptable flow rate per outlet. Note that pumping capacity and pressure are inversely related: Meaning when one goes up, the other goes down.

Example:
Under normal conditions, a pump can produce 10 gpm at 20 psi. If you are using two water consuming appliances, each will receive 5 gpm of water. If we increase the pressure to 30 psi, we might end up with only 6 gpm, which means 3 gpm per appliance.

Conclusion:
An increase in pressure, caused a lower flow rate in gpm at each water using appliance. Sizing and installing a well pump can be a complex process and since pumps are not

cheap it's best to consult a licensed professional who can guarantee the right pump for your needs.

Home Water Treatment Setup

Once you have a pump installed you can consider designing a complete home water treatment system. The main aim of such a system is:

- To feed the interior plumbing with water from your holding tank.

- To filter and purify incoming water for domestic needs.

- To provide a maintenance platform for your water's treatment.

Before you design such a system, you will have to determine your budget, how much energy (power) is available, and which contaminants need to be removed from your water.

Filters. You can use a system of pre- and post-filters to get rid of sediment and other contaminants. Filters come with either a mesh or a micron rating.

A wire mesh system indicates how many openings there are in one inch of screen. It can vary from inch to inch and is not very accurate.

A micron system is more accurate and represents the actual pore size of the filter; 1 micron (1μ) = 0.001 mm.

Basic Home Purifying System

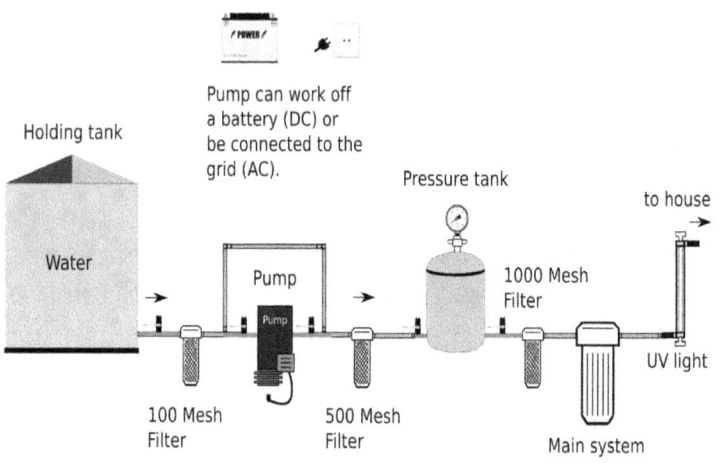

Filter options
1. Standard 100/ 500/ 1000 mesh.
2. Fine 20/ 5/ <1 micron.

Main system options:
1. Ceramic candle filter
2. Reverse osmosis sytem
3. Carbon filter

Filters calibrated in microns are intended to catch very fine particles of minute size. They are normally used at the end of the water line, before your water enters the indoor plumbing. The main thing with filters is that they slow down the flow of the water as it moves though the water line. This puts pressure on your pump and all the other treatment systems. To alleviate the influence of filters, most domestic systems place the largest filters (big pore size) first in the water line and the smallest ones last.

In a standard setup, we find that the first filter is a filter with large pores which will catch larger particles. A simple spin down filter of 100 mesh will do. A 20 micron filter will work for a system dealing with finer particles. This pre-filter will need cleaning often.

You will need a **booster pump** to provide water to the appliances in your house. It should provide between 30 and 80 psi of pressure for optimum results. An automatic pressure sensor will regulate the on and off cycle of the pump.

A DC pump is very economical and only uses electricity when in use. These on-demand pumps are very energy-efficient and you can run it off a battery if needed.

An AC pump will also work, but uses more power.

Make sure that you have stop valves on entrance and exit points of your pump to allow for maintenance when needed.

The second filter catches slighter smaller particles and although the water is not potable yet, it should be clear of visible sediment. At this point in the feed line, the water can be diverted to showers, toilets and washing machines, except if you have known pathogens in your water that have to be removed.

Next in line is your **pressure tank** that will provide pressure to the indoor plumbing and minimize pump usage. Make sure you size your tank according to your pump specifications.

The third filter should be the final one that takes care of all sediment. The water should be clear of hard particles and only dissolved chemicals and pathogens will require removal from here on out.

You **main water treatment system** can be a ceramic candle filter, a reverse osmosis system or a specific filter for your individual needs. It should render your water safe to drink and give you the peace of mind to use it on a daily basis with confidence.

Finally, a **UV light** can also be considered to get rid of viruses. When utilizing such a light, first make sure that all sediment has been removed, for pathogens can hide behind particles and bubbles causes by turbulence. If specific impurities like dissolved chemicals need to be removed, then specialized filters can be employed in the final stage the treatment process.

CHAPTER 05

The Basics Of Managing A Well

Keep in mind that a well is an investment that can last for years if properly taken care of. From "day one" you will have to be involved in the whole process of creating a sustainable well with a healthy life-expectancy. Start with simple observations, measurements and calculations.

a.) While under construction keep notes of time of year, water table depth, soil quality and yield.

b.) Once your well is up and running keep records on productivity, seasonal fluctuations, water testing and general maintenance.

These basic observations will provide you with the information to keep contaminants out of your well and also to prevent your well from running dry due to over-pumping. Managing your well means that you will also have to be prepared in case a flood event or an environmental disaster strikes your area. These are unexpected events and they usually catch

Managing Your Well

No matter which method you used to create your well, you still have to manage and maintain the structure.

Well maintenance can protect your investment , prolong the life of your well and also protect you and your family against possible contaminants.

people off guard, but by simply being prepared, the impact on your water supply can be minimized. The responsibility to manage a well lies squarely on the shoulders of the owner. A well can cause problems on many levels not just for the owners, but also for members of the surrounding community.
Remember that your well uses the same local groundwater as your neighbors and that your actions will affect other groundwater users as well.

Protect Your Well

According to the Centers for Disease Control and Prevention (CDC), here are some steps you can take to help protect your well:

- Wells should be checked and tested ANNUALLY for mechanical problems, cleanliness, and the presence of certain contaminants, such as coliform bacteria, nitrates/nitrites, and any other contaminants of local concern, (for example, arsenic and radon).

• Well water should be tested more than once a year if there are recurrent incidents of gastrointestinal illness among household members or visitors and/or a change in taste, odor, or appearance of the well water.

• All hazardous materials, such as paint, fertilizer, pesticides, and motor oil, should be kept far away from your well.

• When mixing chemicals, do not put the hose inside the mixing container, as this can siphon chemicals into a household's water system.

• Consult a professional contractor to verify that there is proper separation between your well, home, waste systems, and chemical storage facilities.

• Always check the well cover or well cap to ensure it is intact. The top of the well should be at least one foot above the ground.

Call An Expert

Along with the points previously listed, the following are indicators of when a water well systems professional should be called to evaluate the condition of your well:

1. Anytime that the well cap or seal has to be removed to look inside the well.

2. If you experience taste or odor problems, then you should contact a professional to have your water tested

3. If you experience turbidity or cloudiness of water caused by presence of suspended matter ("dirty" looking).

4. If there is a loss of capacity or pressure—the well is not producing as much water as previously produced, the pressure drops and surges, or the pump cycles on and off frequently.

5. If a test is positive for total coliforms, anaerobic bacteria, or any positive test results indicating a potential health concern. Contact a professional or your local or state regulatory agency if you experience any positive test results or believe your well has been contaminated. A water well systems professional should be hired to thoroughly clean and disinfect any well that has had a positive "anaerobic" bacterial test result, which should include removal of any pumping equipment and evacuation of the well to its bottom to be sure of maximum removal of anaerobic growth.

6. When you find defects with your wellhead, the wellhead area, or the overall water system during your routine inspections and find that you do not have the proper tools and/or knowledge to fix the issue(s). A mistake in self-servicing your well can cost you thousands of dollars, cause personal injury or death, damage personal property, and leave you and your family without water until a qualified contractor can be on-site to fix the issue(s).

Once your well has reached its serviceable life, have a licensed or certified water well driller and pump installer decommission the existing well and construct a new well. Never dispose of any chemicals or organic waste inside your old, decommissioned well.

Visual Inspections

According to the National Ground Water Association, to monitor your well's performance, you will have to carry out specific visual inspections:

• The Well Casing (pipe protruding from the ground) must be examined. Check the general condition and check if the casing extends at least 12 inches above ground. If not, hire a qualified professional to investigate remedial action.

• The Well Cap (cap on top of casing) must be present. Check the condition of the cap and any seals present, that it is securely attached, and that it will keep out insects and rodents. If not, hire a qualified professional to repair or replace the well cap.

• Survey the area above ground, surrounding the well. Check the location relative to potential sources of contamination, flooding, and physical dangers. Look for chemicals such as paint, fertilizer, pesticides, or motor oil. Remove all unwanted contaminants if possible.

• It is important to maintain at least 100 feet between the well and any kennels, pastures, feeding areas, or livestock operations.

Ensure a proper distance is maintained from buildings, waste systems, or chemical storage areas (including fuel tanks)—a water well systems professional should know local codes and requirements. If there is any concern, contact your water well systems professional or your local health department.

Annual Water Well Checkup

The National Ground Water Association suggests that at a minimum, wells should be evaluated annually by a licensed or certified water well systems professional.

An annual water well checkup should include:

• A flow test.

• A visual inspection.

• A water quality test for coliform and anaerobic bacteria, nitrates, and anything else of local concern.

• Checking of valves.

• Performing electrical testing.

A written report should be delivered to you following completion of an annual checkup. The report should include recommendations and all laboratory and other test results. Keep this in a safe place with all other well reports.

- The ground surrounding the wellhead should slope away towards a storm-water drain. This is to divert any surface water run-off and to prevent contamination. If not, consider allowing for the ground to slope away from the well casing, while maintaining a proper height of the casing above the ground. A water well systems professional can extend the height of the casing if needed.

- You should have a concrete apron around your well casing. If there is no concrete pad surrounding the well casing, contact your local health department or regulatory agency to determine if one should be installed by a water well systems professional.

- If the well is equipped with a vented well cap, check for the presence of the vent screen in the well vent, and clear away any debris that has accumulated on the vent screen. Check the condition of the vent screen to ensure it can prevent insects and animals from entering.

- Any growth of weeds, trees, shrubs, or grasses with root systems within 10 feet of the well should be physically removed.

- Avoid the use of chemicals or herbicides near the wellhead.

- The well should not be in a roadway or driveway. If it is within close proximity to a roadway or driveway, it should be properly marked to avoid being hit by vehicles. You can protect your well by placing bollards or bump posts near the well's vulnerable position(s) to increase visibility.

• Special care should be observed if your well is located near a driveway and you live where it snows. Wells easily disappear below snow cover and are easily overlooked when pushing snow takes place.

• Be conscious of any other potential threats to the wellhead—garages, ATVs, sledding hills, debris, dirt, surface water, fuels and chemicals (including fertilizers), and runoff water from kennels, pastures, or feedlots.

• Keep the well out of dog runs or animal pens.

• If your well is located in a low-lying area prone to flooding, you should consider having your water well systems professional raise the well casing to at least 12 inches above the historic record flood level, properly sealing the wiring conduit and providing casing bump protection if floating debris is a concern.

Another option is to construct a new well at a location outside the flood-prone area.

Disinfecting A Well

The Centers for Disease Control and Prevention (CDC) made the following guidelines available to the public, concerning well disinfection after an emergency. Don't forget that plugging or capping your well before a disaster is a great way of preventing or reducing contamination.

If extensive flooding has occurred or you suspect that the well may be contaminated, **DO NOT** drink the water. Use a safe water supply like bottled or treated water.

Safety Precautions

The following safety precautions must be followed before you can disinfect your well:

1. Inspect the area around the well. Remove suspected contaminants that are visible.

2. Turn off all electricity to the well. Don't attempt to fix any machinery if not qualified.

3. Clear hazards away from the well.

4. Do not enter the well pit. Gases and vapors can build up in well pits, creating a hazardous environment.

5. Wear protective goggles or a face shield when working with chlorine solutions.

6. When mixing and handling chlorine solutions, work in well-ventilated areas and avoid breathing vapors.

7. Warn users not to drink or bathe in water until all the well disinfection steps have been completed.

How To Disinfect A Well

To disinfect your well, follow these steps:

1. If the well is equipped with an electrical pump, turn off all electricity and clear debris from around the top of the well.

Repair the electrical system and pump if needed. Contact a qualified electrician, well contractor, or pump contractor if you are not experienced with this type of work.

2. Start the pump and run the water until it is clear. Use the outside faucet nearest to the well to drain the potentially contaminated water from the well and keep the unsafe well water out of the interior household plumbing. If no pump is installed, bail water from the well with a bucket or other device until the water is clear.

If the well is connected to interior home plumbing, close valves to any water softener units.

3. Use the Tables (Imperial and Metric) on the next page to determine the amount of liquid household bleach needed to disinfect the well. Use only unscented bleach.

4. Using a 5-gallon bucket, mix the bleach from the Table with 3-5 gallons of water (12-19L).

5. Remove the vent cap. Pour the bleach water mixture into the well using a funnel. Avoid all electrical connections. Attach a clean hose to the nearest hose bib and use it to circulate water back into the well for thorough mixing.

6. Rinse the inside of the well casing with a garden hose or bucket for 5-10 minutes.

7. Open all faucets inside the home and run the water until you notice a strong odor of chlorine (bleach) at each faucet. Turn off all faucets and allow the solution to remain in the well and plumbing for a minimum of 12 hours.

8. After at least 12 hours, attach a hose to an outside faucet and drain the chlorinated water onto a non-vegetated area such as a driveway or storm water drain. Continue draining until the chlorine odor disappears. Avoid draining into open sources of water (streams, ponds, etc.).

9. Turn on all indoor faucets and run water until the chlorine odor disappears.

10. Wait at least 7-10 days after disinfection, then have the water in your well sampled. Water sampling cannot be done until all traces of chlorine have been flushed from the system.

11. Sample the water for total coliform and either E. Coli or fecal coliform bacteria to confirm that the water is safe to drink.

If the results show no presence of total coliforms or fecal coliforms, the water can be considered safe to drink from a microbial standpoint.

Follow up with two additional samples, one in the next 2 to 4 weeks and another in 3 to 4 months.

12. Check the safety of your water over the long term, continue to monitor bacterial quality at least twice per year or more often if you suspect any changes in your water quality.

If results show the presence of any coliform bacteria, repeat the well disinfection process and re-sample. If tests continue to show the presence of bacteria, contact your local health department for assistance.

Take note!
Fuel and other chemical releases and spills are common during flood events. If your water smells like fuel, has a chemical odor or if you live in an area where the potential for a release of fuels, pesticides, or chemicals is high, contact your local health department for advice.
Water contaminated with chemicals will not be made safe by boiling or disinfection.
Until you know the water is safe, use bottled water or some other safe supply of water.

Disinfecting A Drilled/ Driven Well (Imperial)

- Use only unscented household liquid chlorine bleach.
- Bleach concentrations are generally 5% - 8.25%.
- Quantities given in this table are approximate and are rounded to the nearest practical measurement.
- Amounts given are calculated in accordance with reaching a chlorine concentration of >100 mg/L.

Key to abbreviations:

1 cup = 8 fluid ounces = 16 tablespoons (tbsp)

1 gallon (gal) = 16 cups

Well Disinfection Table: Approximate mount Of Bleach

Depth of water	Inside Diameter of Well Casing (Inches)						
	2"	4"	6"	8"	10"	24"	36"
10 feet	$3/4$ tbsp	$3 1/4$ tbsp	$1/2$ cup	$3/4$ cup	$1 1/4$ cup	7 cup	1 gal
20 feet	$1 1/2$ tbsp	$6 1/2$ tbsp	1 cup	$1 1/2$ cup	$2 1/2$ cup	14 cup	2 gal
30 feet	$2 1/4$ tbsp	$9 3/4$ tbsp	$1 1/2$ cup	$2 1/4$ cup	$3 3/4$ cup	$1 1/4$ gal	3 gal
40 feet	3 tbsp	13 tbsp	2 cup	3 cup	5 cup	$1 3/4$ gal	4 gal
50 feet	$3 3/4$ tbsp	1 cup	$2 1/2$ cup	$3 3/4$ cup	$6 1/4$ cup	$2 1/4$ gal	5 gal
100	$7 1/2$ tbsp	2 cup	5 cup	$7 1/2$ cup	$12 1/2$ cup	$4 1/2$ gal	10 gal

The Basics Of Managing A Well

Disinfecting A Drilled/ Driven Well (Metric)
- Use only unscented household liquid chlorine bleach.
- Bleach concentrations are generally 5% - 8.25%.
- Quantities given in this table are approximate and are rounded to the nearest practical measurement.
- Amounts given are calculated in accordance with reaching a chlorine concentration of >100 mg/L.

Key to abbreviations:

1 meter (m) = 100 centimeters (cm)

1 liter (L) = 1000 milliliters (ml)

Well Disinfection Table: Approximate Amount Of Bleach

Depth of water	Inside Diameter of Well Casing (Centimeters)						
	5cm	10cm	15cm	20cm	25cm	60cm	90cm
3m	12ml	48ml	118ml	177ml	296ml	1.66L	3.78L
6m	24ml	96ml	236ml	354ml	592ml	3.32L	7.56L
9m	36ml	144ml	354ml	531ml	888ml	4.98L	11.34L
12m	48ml	192ml	472ml	708ml	1.18L	6.64L	15.12L
15m	60ml	240ml	590ml	885ml	1.48L	8.3L	18.9L
30m	120ml	480ml	1.18L	1.77L	2.96L	16.6L	37.8L

Disinfecting A Dug Well (Imperial)

- Use only unscented household liquid chlorine bleach.
- Bleach concentrations are generally 5% - 8.25%.
- Quantities given in this table are approximate and are rounded to the nearest practical measurement.
- Amounts given are calculated in accordance with reaching a chlorine concentration of >100 mg/L.

Key to abbreviations:

1 cup = 8 fluid ounces = 16 tablespoons (tbsp)
1 gallon (gal) = 16 cups

Well Disinfection Table: Approximate mount Of Bleach

Depth of water	Inside Diameter of Well Casing (Feet)					
	0.5'	1'	2'	3'	4'	5'
10 feet	1/2 cup	1 3/4 cup	7 cup	1 gal	1 3/4 gal	2 3/4 gal
20 feet	1 cup	3 1/2 cup	14 cup	2 gal	3 1/2 gal	5 1/2 gal
30 feet	1 1/2 cup	5 1/4 cup	1 1/4 gal	3 gal	5 1/4 gal	8 1/4 gal
40 feet	2 cup	7 cup	1 3/4 gal	4 gal	7 gal	11 gal
50 feet	2 1/2 cup	8 3/4 cup	2 1/4 gal	5 gal	8 3/4 gal	13 3/4 gal

The Basics Of Managing A Well

Disinfecting A Dug Well (Metric)

- Use only unscented household liquid chlorine bleach.
- Bleach concentrations are generally 5% - 8.25%.
- Quantities given in this table are approximate and are rounded to the nearest practical measurement.
- Amounts given are calculated in accordance with reaching a chlorine concentration of >100 mg/L.

Key to abbreviations:

1 meter (m) = 100 centimeters (cm)

1 liter (L) = 1000 milliliters (ml)

Well Disinfection Table:
Approximate Amount Of Bleach

Depth of water	Inside Diameter of Well Casing (Meters)					
	0.15m	0.3m	0.6m	0.9m	1.2m	1.5m
3m	118ml	414ml	1.66L	3.78L	6.62L	10.41L
6m	236ml	828ml	3.32L	7.56L	13.24L	20.82L
9m	354ml	1.24L	4.98L	11.34L	19.86L	31.23L
12m	472ml	2.49L	6.64L	15.12L	26.48L	41.64L
15m	590ml	3.72L	8.3L	18.9L	33.10L	52.05L

GLOSSARY

Cavitation. The formation of bubbles in a liquid, typically by the movement of a propeller through it.

Check valve. A valve that closes to prevent backward flow of liquid.

Foot valve. A one-way valve at the inlet of a pipe or the base of a suction pump.

Pressure switch. A switch that automatically turns water on and off, depending on pressure settings.

Pressure tank. A tank in which a liquid or gas is stored under pressure greater than atmospheric. This helps maintain water pressure to keep appliances running efficiently.

Depth to water. The distance measured from the ground level to the water level in the well when the pump is not in operation.

Draw down. Amount of usable water we can get out of the water pressure tank before the pump has to turn on

Draw down water level. The distance from ground level to the water level inside the well, while water is being pumped from the well.

Well capacity (gpm). The amount of water measured in gallons per minute that the well produces without the water level dropping.

Well total depth. The distance measured from the ground level down to the bottom of the well.

Apron. A reinforced concrete floor all around the top of the well. It prevents contaminants from entering the well.

Caisson ring. A watertight retaining structure used on the foundations of a bridge pier, for the construction of a concrete dam, or for the repair of ships.

Concrete. A mixture of cement, sand and gravel.

Windlass. A type of winch used to lower buckets into and hoist them up from wells.

Aquifer. A geological formation that contains or conducts groundwater, especially one that supplies water for wells and springs.

Auger. A hand-held tool consisting of a twisted rod of metal (drill bit) attached to a handle, used for making holes in the soil.

Groundwater. The water that collects/ flows beneath the earth's surface, like porous spaces in soil, sediment and rock.

Standing water level. SWL refers to the level of the water in a well, in a normal rest position when undisturbed and under no-pumping conditions.

Water table. The upper level of an underground surface in which the soil or rocks are permanently saturated with water.

Well screen. A filtering device, placed at the bottom of the well, that allows water to enter from the aquifer, but prevents sediment from entering the well.

Well point. A well screen with a forged-steel point and a threaded pipe shank at the top end. Usually 1.25-2" thick. Driven into the ground with a sledgehammer.

Well casing. A tubular casing made of plastic or metal and placed inside a well bore-hole to maintain the well opening.

INDEX

Index
A
Add extra pipe 52
alternative water source 19
Annual Water Well Checkup 134
Apron 145
Aquifer 146
Auger 146
Auger Drilling 62
B
Basic Home Purifying System 126
Benefits of using precast concrete rings 96
C
Caisson ring 146
Call An Expert 131
Cavitation 145
Check valve 145
Check Valves And Foot Valves 103
closed hydrological system 4
Concrete 146
condenses 4
Connecting An Electric Pump 102
Connecting A Solar Water Pump 116
Conservation 8
Construct Your Drill 42
D
Digging your own well 27
Disinfecting A Drilled Or Driven Well (Imperial) 141, 143
Disinfecting A Drilled Or Driven Well (Metric) 142, 144
Disinfecting A Well 136
Draw down 145
Draw down water level 145
Drilling a well yourself 27
drill pipe 38
drill tip 38
Driving a well point 28
Dug Wells 82
Dug Wells and Safety Concerns 99
E
evaporation 4
Extracting Water From The Ground
Clay 31
Get Legal 34
Gravel 29
Plan the type of well you want 35
Research 32
Rock 31
Sand 29
The Soil 29
The Water Table 31
F
Flexible coupling 47
Foot valve 145
G
General Pump Maintenance 122
Get Legal 34
Groundwater 146
H
Hire a professional 28
Home Water Treatment Set-up 125
How To Dig And Construct A Well 82
How To Dig And Construct A Well Using An Auger 62
How To Dig And Construct A Well Using A Well Point 72
How To Disinfect A Well 137
How To Drill And Construct A Well Using PVC Pipe 36
How to lower concrete rings in a level position 95
How to make a well-screen 68
How to pour pea gravel around the well screen 60
How will you know when you've hit water? 54
I
Installation and priming 110
L
Local Community Water. 18
M
Make a PVC bail bucket 70
municipal water 13
P
Pitless Adapters 107
Plan the type of well you want 35
Point Wells 72

Pressure switch 145
Pressure tank 145
Pressure Tanks 104
Protect Your Well 129
Public Water 15
Pump Basics 103
PVC Cross Tee 44
PVC Valve 45

Q
Questions to ask a licensed well driller 22

R
Reducer bushings 45
Research 32

S
Solar Pump Basics 1 118
Solar Pump Basics 2 119
Solar Pump Basics 3 119, 121
Solar Pump Basics 4 122
Spring Water 17
Standing water level 146

T
The Basics Of A Deep Well Jet Pump 111
The Basics Of A Shallow Well Jet Pump 108
The Basics Of A Submersible Deep Well Pump 113
The Basics Of Managing A Well
Call An Expert 131
Visual Inspections 133
The Basics of Wells And Water Pumps
Check Valves And Foot Valves 103
Connecting An Electric Pump 102
Connecting A Solar Water Pump 116
General Pump Maintenance 122
Pitless Adapters 107
Pressure Tanks 104
Pump Basics 103
Solar Pump Basics 1 118
Solar Pump Basics 2 119
Solar Pump Basics 3 121
Solar Pump Basics 4 122
The Basics Of A Deep Well Jet Pump 111
The Basics Of A Shallow Well Jet Pump 108
The Basics Of A Submersible Deep Well Pump 113
The Drill Bit 49
The Drill Handle Bar 50
The Drill Top 42
The Main Water Line. 16
The Origins Of Water
condenses 4
Conservation 8
Global Water Crisis 5
The Water Cycle 3
Water and Droughts 7
water vapor 4
The Soil 29
The use of well water. 37
The Water Cycle 3
The Water Table 31
The well screen 55
torque arrestor 116

U
Using an auger to drill your well 28

V
Visual Inspections 133

W
Water and Droughts 7
Water Bearing Layers 30
Water table 146
water vapor 4
Well basics 27
Well capacity 145
well casing 38
Well casing 146
Well Drilling Basics 40
Well point 146
Well screen 146
Well total depth 145
Windlass 146

Y
Your Water Rights 23

About The Author

Daniel Schoeman is a scholar and researcher of languages, cultures, carpentry, plumbing, construction, agriculture and how to live off the land.

He first started traveling the planet in 1997 and worked as a willing worker on organic farms in Australia. His journey has since taken him to a variety of locales all over the world and given him the privilege to see how different cultures live and deal with their respective environments.

His motivation stems from an aspiration to create a world where self-sufficient, off the grid living is endorsed, and where housing can be affordable to all humans with the will and determination to work for it.

His latest endeavor is researching and writing how-to articles on welding, and also on the construction of steel and glass designed houses.

This is his third resource guide on Prepping.

www.ingramcontent.com/pod-product-compliance
Lightning Source LLC
Chambersburg PA
CBHW071402290426
44108CB00014B/1651